PAWPRINTS ON THE HEART

PAWPRINTS
ON THE
HEART

Healing From Pet Loss Grief and
Cultivating the Unbreakable Bond
With Your Furry Friend

NOLAN SANDS

Published by

www.headuppress.com

Dedication

I will never forget the day Maqui came into my life. I was going through a difficult stage, full of disappointments. Then she arrived, transforming the pain into something small and insignificant. From the first moment we met, I knew our connection would be immense. Maqui became my family, my home, and my partner in adventure. She was, in every way, part of me.

Maqui had a fascinating duality: surly with strangers but tender with those she met, capable of softening any heart. Together we lived in a beach-front apartment where her daily expeditions made it clear that the city was not enough for her bold essence. She hunted lizards, caught moths, jumped from rock to rock, and efficiently ran through the dunes. Maqui was, by nature, wilder than other dogs.

During the COVID-19 pandemic, I moved from the city to the country, which allowed me to establish an ecological refuge on the banks of a beautiful river. We traded city lights for endless green landscapes, and she became the queen of our new home. The adaptability, flexibility, and authenticity lessons that Maqui taught me during that time were invaluable.

On a Tuesday, abruptly and tragically, Maqui left this world. The pain I felt when I found her in that ditch after chasing a rabbit cannot be explained. Her absence has left a hole in my life, and every day without her is challenging. It pains me to know that I will never again be able to see her run, hug, and hold her in my arms.

To honor her memory, I decided to scatter her ashes in her favorite places, where I have memories of seeing her enjoying herself immensely. Maqui, I will be infinitely grateful for the love and companionship you gave me. I will never forget your brave spirit, loyalty, and passion for life.

Although the loss of Maqui still hurts, I am grateful for the time we shared. This unique bond made me feel complete and allowed me to experience a love that I would describe as highly pure. Despite the pain, I hope we will meet again in this or another life. I am comforted by the thought that, in some way, she is still with me.

I love and miss you, Maqui, my traveling star.

For all those who have gone through or are currently going through a similar situation, I share with you a phrase that resonated with me when I read it: *"If having a soul means being able to feel love and loyalty and gratitude, then animals are better off than a lot of humans."* — James Herriot.

Table of Contents

Welcome!

We are so happy that you have decided to begin your journey toward healing from your beloved pet's grief.

As a token of our appreciation, **we would like to give you a FREE GIFT**: an *article* about the _role our pets play in the emotional development of our children_.

The Furry Factor
Boosting Emotional Intelligence Development In Children

To claim your gift, scan the QR code or enter the URL in your favorite browser:

gifts.headuppress.com/TFF

We wish you all the best in the healing process you are about to begin.

Sincerely,
The Head Up Press Team

Introduction

*"An animal's eyes have the power to
speak a great language."*

—Martin Buber

Anyone can be a pet owner, but it takes a special kind of love to be a pet parent. You can even say that pet owners are pet lovers, right? So, how are pet parents different from pet lovers?

A pet owner will occasionally take a selfie with their pet, whereas a pet parent will have complete albums and collages of them and their pet doing practically everything together. Yes, they are so utterly interconnected. A typical pet owner is someone who loves all animals. Since they are animals, they have a propensity to be drawn to these animal lovers. On the other hand, pet parents share this inclination but also have a personal preference toward their own animals. They consider their dogs, cats, or whatever pet they own to be the best ever, and everything else is nothing special in comparison.

This holds true even if an animal they have been admiring at the time may have won some award. Despite the facts, they always have their hearts firmly fixed on the biased belief that their pet is the best in the world!

Although any vet listed in a pet owner's address book would suffice to schedule an appointment, pet parents will go to tremendous measures to find their pet the best veterinarian. To ensure that their pet receives the most individualized treatment possible, they make sure to have a personal relationship with this veterinarian (they even have them on speed dial).

You are a pet parent if you are the kind who visits the veterinarian using your pet's insurance. You value your pet and care about ensuring they receive the best possible treatment without having to worry about money since you have taken out a health insurance policy for them.

Pet lovers can endure animal movies with tragic endings, even though they are difficult for them to watch. When a pet parent sees a movie about a pet that has a sad ending, they typically sob uncontrollably or decide not to watch it at all.

Let's talk about personal space. If you wanted the entire space to yourself, would you ever kick your kid out of your bed? The likelihood is high that you wouldn't. Even though you'll be careful to establish limits, you'll always allow the baby to sleep with you if they come to your bedroom because they're afraid of the thunder, had a nightmare, or simply can't go to sleep without you. Parents behave in this way. It's natural.

Pet owners are not affected by this issue. Their canines are not permitted on the furniture, let alone on their beds. As a result, they can go to sleep confident that Beethoven won't charge in and insist on sleeping in that cozy spot right in the middle of the bed. On the other hand, pet parents are unable to remember the last time they had the couch or the bed to themselves. They love having their pet children with them, whenever possible.

So, how do you relate? Are you a pet owner or a pet parent? Since you are reading this, I think it is safe to assume you are the latter.

I am a proud and loving pet parent, and although I know not *everyone* will understand, my love is so great for my pets that I want to shout it from the rooftops!

Only pet parents can appreciate and enjoy the full being of their pets. We know that each pet we ever had has their own personality. No two pets are the same. Whether they are cats, dogs, birds, or any other pet, their behaviors, interests, and reactions differ. Mere pet owners don't recognize this. Would you agree?

I'll admit, I pity those who do not see the power pets have of speaking a great language when you look into their eyes. When you have such a deep and rich love that only a pet parent can have, you experience things that are mostly invisible to the outside world. Your pets know when you're excited because they react in kind. But they also know when you are sad. Have you ever felt downcast when your dog comes close, trying their best to comfort you? I'm sure most of us, if not all, have experienced this.

But, as beautiful and powerful as this is, therein also lies the dilemma. Our pets don't live forever, even if we wish they had. As strong as our bonds are with our pets, when the day comes for them to leave us, it creates a dark and painful hole in our souls. And because every pet is so unique with their own personality, it feels impossible to fill that hole, or even to heal. How can I go on with a love for life without my beloved pet? How can I ever be excited again, knowing they won't be wagging their tail or sharing in my joy?

My dear friend, I will not pretend to know exactly what you're going through. Since our pets are so individually unique. Moreover, I believe that the pain we feel after losing them is also unique. However, since we all share this one thing—an undeniable and great love for our pets—I can say this: There is healing. It may take time and it may be difficult, but you will smile again when you remember your beloved pet.

I have learned that we *never* merely accept, forget, and move on from who we have lost. That pet will have a special place forever, and it should be no different! In this book, I will walk with you toward healing. We'll talk about remembering and honoring your pet, and how you can face the world again in their sweet remembrance.

We'll embark on this journey from the start—exploring the human-animal bond and why it is so powerful, the different types of pet loss and how to effectively deal with it, and why the heartache feels so unbearable. We'll also talk about how you can help children deal with the loss of a beloved pet.

Then, we'll discuss the grieving process and what you can expect. You can expect that it will be difficult, and there's nothing wrong with that! Losing a loved one, including pets, is hard and unimaginable. So, whatever emotions you're experiencing, never suppress them for fear that others won't understand. The point is, this is *your* experience. Even if others can't comprehend what you're going through, you have to walk this path. But now, you won't be alone. I'll be with you, every step of the way.

Of course, self-care is vital during this process. It feels like life has placed a brick wall right in front of you, making it feel like you can't move forward. But this doesn't mean you shouldn't take care of yourself anymore. It's more than essential during this time. Eventually, we'll smash through that wall anyway, and you'll feel the warmth of the sun on your face once again.

Many pet parents find that many bricks in this wall are made up of guilt. Feeling remorseful and guilty are things that most of us experience when we lose a pet. Don't fear, we'll talk about that too and explore ways in which you can overcome it. We'll also talk about ways you can honor and commemorate your pet. Their passing does not need to remain dark and gloomy. We have the opportunity of allowing the beauty of their existence to last, even when they had to leave this world.

Are you ready to start this journey? We won't rush. The path to healing will be gentle and paved with love. Together, we'll remember and honor the memory of our pets, while feeling grateful for the pawprints they left on our hearts.

1

Tale as Old as Time – The Bonding Between a Human and Their Pet

"We are born in relationships, wounded in relationships, and heal in relationships."

—Harville Hendrix

Losing a pet will never be easy, given that they share so much with their owners. This viewpoint makes it simple to comprehend the severe suffering that may come with the loss of a pet. Although it is not often apparent to others, intense grieving at such a loss is normal and natural. Sorrow, following the death of a pet can be quite similar to that experienced with the loss of a human loved one. Even though people handle loss in different ways, these emotions can remain extremely difficult to bear.

Nevertheless, mourning over the passing or other loss of an animal is not typically accepted in society. People who are grieving the loss of a pet do not receive the ritualized comfort that we provide to those who have lost a close relative. When a loved one passes away, it is normal for people to show their grief in public. The funeral and accompanying rituals bring family members together to support those who are grieving. When a pet dies, there isn't much of this acceptance of mourning. At best, the grieving individual can be viewed as weak or juvenile. Pet funerals and burials are often not treated with care, and many owners do not receive true condolences.

Some things could deepen someone's grief over losing a pet. These factors include the degree of the owner's attachment to the pet (which is the focal point of this chapter), the nature of the loss or death, the owner's own experience of losses, and their social support or religious convictions. Accepting the sadness, pain, guilt, rage, and other emotions is essential when coping with the loss of a cherished pet.

To process these emotions and move toward healing, it is useful to analyze and accept them. First and foremost, one must accept their grief; the loss of love, affection, and camaraderie is profound. It can be incredibly helpful to process your grief with the help of a family member, close friend, or counselor. Putting things into perspective and figuring out how to deal with the challenging emotions as they arise can both be achieved by having a caring conversation. Being able to talk about your pet and how much you miss and value them is beneficial. Writing in a notebook, browsing through photos, or taking some time to reflect on the various emotions and memories that surface are all beneficial ways for people to express themselves.

Let's talk about the foundation of your love and other emotions—the human-animal bond.

WHAT IS THE HUMAN-ANIMAL BOND?

As animal lovers, we are deeply entwined with animals in both our personal and professional lives. The physiology, diet, genetics, management, behavior, and health and disease of companions, laboratory, and exotic animals as well as wildlife are all studied by humans. This section examines the relationship between people and animals as well as the domestication of cattle and dogs from their earliest forms to the present.

The investigation of the link between humans and animals, or our psychological and social interactions with them, is a true scientific animal frontier. The nature of our psychological and social relationships with the creatures that share our planet is one of the more recent animal frontiers that is being investigated. Leo Bustad and Michael McCulloch first used the phrase "human-animal bond" in the latter part of the 1970s. The Delta Society, which seeks to comprehend the interrelationship between animals, people, and the environment, had just been established by Drs. Bustad and McCulloch (Hines, 2003).

The human-animal bond has different behavioral, psychological, physiological, ecological, social, and ethical effects than when either partner exists alone, and this relationship is now being recognized as a scientific discipline. The renewed dedication to animal welfare is a result of both our increased awareness of animals' needs and our growing understanding of the varied roles they play in our lives. But we must keep in mind that for there to be a "bond," the impact on each partner must be positive and secure. In fact, the relationship between people and the animals they own is important and mutually beneficial, especially since they protect one another and provide emotional care and support, among other things.

The pet sector saw its fair share of impact and development in the year 2020. The American Pet Products Association's (APPA) 2020 State of the Industry Report stated that the sector's sales crossed the $100 billion mark for the first time in the recorded year. The APPA predicted growth of 5.8% for the next year, which is significantly higher than the 3% to 4% historical average.

The number of households in the United States that own some kind of pet has increased from 67% in the 2019-2020 survey to 70% in the 2021–2022 APPA National Pet Owners Survey. A total of 14% of all respondents (pet owners and non-pet owners combined) got a new pet during the pandemic, and at least one in four of those who just got a pet claimed the pandemic had an impact on their decision (APPA, 2021).

Why Animals?

Around 10,000 years ago, humans in Mesopotamia first domesticated animals for their milk, meat, and hides. Animal hides and skins were utilized to construct tent huts and for clothing and storage. Sheep and goats were probably the first two species to be domesticated. Around the same time, chickens were domesticated in Southeast Asia. Larger animals, like oxen or horses, were later tamed by humans for use in transportation and plowing. We refer to these as beasts of burden.

Animal domestication can be a challenging job. Because they are the easiest to feed, herbivorous animals that graze on greenery are the simplest to domesticate. For instance, domesticating cows is easier. Because grains are valuable and may therefore need to be domesticated, it is more challenging to domesticate herbivores that consume them than herbivores that graze. For instance, chickens can live on grains and seeds.

People have bred such animals for specific traits throughout history. Domestic animals are chosen for their calm disposition and propensity to reproduce in confinement. Their capacity to fend off sickness and endure in hostile environments is also advantageous.

These characteristics gradually distinguish farmed animals from their wild counterparts. The selective breeding of dogs most likely began with gray wolves. Gray wolves and dogs are different species now. The weight of early wild chickens was around two pounds. But they have been bred to be bigger throughout their hundreds of years of domestication. More meat is produced by larger birds. In current times, chickens can now weigh up to 17 pounds. While chickens typically lay 200 or more eggs each year, wild chickens only produce a tiny number of eggs per year.

Why Do People Love Their Pets So Much?

Some animals that were tamed for a certain use started to exist beyond that purpose. For example, some dogs were domesticated to help people with hunting. Today, there are countless varieties of dogs. Although most of them are pets, many of them are still skilled hunters. This had a great effect on the relationship between people and domesticated animals.

When we discuss our problems and concerns with others, people usually jump right into problem-solving when what we really need is connection, comprehension, and empathy. Most animals, and most dogs in particular, are not only naturally excellent at doing this for us but are also genetically programmed to do so.

It's likely that you already appreciate the delight of returning home to a pet who has spent the entire day anticipating your arrival. How often can human responses equal the emotional expression of a dog when you walk through the door? What we actually want from human connections is to feel genuinely understood, respected, loved, important, and special without condition, which is revealed by our infatuation with pets. This connection can thus be a remedy for loneliness, meaninglessness, and loss, as long as we don't become unduly dependent on our pets and become socially isolated.

Our social circuitry, which prioritizes our innate need for close bonds and connections, is encoded in our brains. Their existence is programmed in our survival code. Before we become independent, we are inherently interdependent. This is visible from the moment of birth when we rely on our attachment figures to fulfill our most basic requirements. Being alone is not how we are designed to be and can be innately traumatic.

The fact that the majority (though not all) of developmental delays in children are caused by their environment and caregivers failing to meet their requirements serves as further evidence of how interconnected humans are. Interestingly, these connections don't have to be between people. For many people, pets may step in when other people are unable to.

In the end, how well we can control ourselves, succeed, and feel comfortable in our skin depends on how well we can form attachment ties with others. Our self-esteem is boosted when we are given special treatment and importance, which pets excel at providing (indeed, this is the most crucial factor in boosting self-esteem!). Pets are ideal in this situation because their primary purpose is to connect with us, understand our emotions, and be available, and caring (a great deal of pet owners know the comfort of having them empathetically try to reassure them).

Yes, pets occasionally urinate on the rug to express their anguish at missing their owner. Pets, however, are innocent of hidden agendas. Other than wanting love, attention, playtime outside, and food, they won't try to manipulate you or gaslight you. They won't ever choose to avoid spending time with you in favor of going to a friend's party. As long as you treat them well (and frequently even if you don't: but do treat them well regardless, they deserve it!), they won't pursue an affair since you are everything to them and they are fervently, wholeheartedly devoted to you.

Animals understand us even when we non-verbally express ourselves. They are emotionally in tune with us and unaffected by words or other complex or nuanced aspects of interpersonal relationships. If communication is a dance, emotion is the melody. For instance, they just love us no matter what; they won't quarrel with us about politics or whose side you're on in the Neil Young, Joe Rogan, and Spotify controversy. Through emotion, we form bonds with our pets and one another.

Pets understand that we are far more emotionally oriented than cognitively, and they take advantage of this to establish close connections with us. The same is fundamental in human relationships. How pets support, comfort, and adore their owners in both their personal and professional lives inspire many of us. They appear to execute it more skillfully than most people do! Loving pets, like the majority of dogs among others, may be a critical missing puzzle piece for busy families, lonely individuals, and persons struggling with mental health issues.

BENEFITS FROM THIS INCREDIBLE HUMAN-ANIMAL BOND

Pets give us companionship and unconditional affection, two things that are getting harder and harder to come by in today's environment. Additionally, they aid in stress and anxiety relief and even improve our mood and mental wellness. The benefits of owning a pet were examined by psychologists at Miami and St. Louis Universities. Their three studies revealed that having a pet can improve both one's physical and mental well-being. During their initial study, it was established that pet owners had higher overall well-being than non-pet owners (McConnell et al., 2011).

Findings From the Healthy Aging Survey by the University of Michigan

Many senior citizens in the United States have pets and view them as members of the family. A person's health and well-being can benefit from having a pet as well as from the companionship they provide. The University of Michigan's National Poll on Healthy Aging surveyed persons nationwide in the age range of 50 to 80 in October 2018 to learn more about their pet ownership, including the positive and negative aspects of doing so (Healthyagingpoll.org, 2019).

A total of 55% of older persons stated that they owned a pet. The majority of pet owners (68%) had dogs, 48% had cats, and 16% had smaller pets like birds, hamsters, or fish. A combined 55% of pet owners said they have more than one pet. Adults aged 50 to 64 were more likely to own a pet than those aged 65 to 80. While 20% of respondents said they looked after their pets on their own, 80% said they had support. Moreover, 53% of pet owners said that their pets sleep in their beds.

Pet owners reported that their animals provide them with a feeling of purpose (73%), alleviate stress (79%), make them feel loved (86%), and help them enjoy life (88%). Additionally, respondents stated that their pets make them feel more socially connected (65%), encourage physical activity (64% overall and 78% of dog owners), and assist them in coping with physical and mental symptoms (60%), including distracting them from pain (34%).

Studies on the Benefits of Having a Pet

An overview of research on the therapeutic use of animals is provided by researchers from Aarhus University in Denmark, Vestfold University College in Norway, and the Swedish University of Agricultural Sciences in Sweden. They also offer some suggestions for how to pinpoint and quantify a potential causal link between animal contact in a therapeutic setting and the long-term effects (Thodberg et al., 2014).

In a 1987 report, the National Institutes of Health stated that "All future studies of human health should consider the presence or absence of a pet in the home and, perhaps, the nature of this relationship with the pet, as a significant variable" (Beck and Meyers, 1996).

Interestingly, researchers from the WALTHAM Centre for Pet Nutrition in the United Kingdom follow the development of research on human-animal interaction, concentrating on studies about interactions with our pets that can provide specific therapeutic value in a variety of contexts and have profound health benefits, including improved cardiovascular health (Griffin et al., 2019).

There are now trained animals that do a number of tasks to help persons with special needs in addition to our everyday contact with animals. From the introduction of the first guide dogs in 1929, Sally Irvin of the Indiana Canine Assistant Network has explored the various functions that animals have fulfilled (Irvin, 2014). The advantages of equine-assisted activities and therapies are also covered by Erika Berg from North Dakota State University and Amy Causey from Horsedust Ltd. in Texas (Berg and Causey, 2014).

Michelle's
STORY

After falling from a tree at the age of 25, Michelle Kephart developed quadriplegia. She was still able to marry a great man and pursue her dream of becoming a nurse. However, it was difficult to work as a full-time quadriplegic nurse. Michelle received assistance from caregivers for two hours in the morning and one hour at night, but otherwise, she was left alone. Working full-time, Michelle's husband came home at odd hours.

Michelle was entirely paralyzed from the waist down and had partial use of her upper extremities due to the fifth cervical vertebrae in her neck being shattered. Her triceps, wrists, and hands were all immobile, yet she could move her shoulders and biceps.

Being in a wheelchair and living alone, Michelle frequently dropped things on the floor and was unable to pick them up. Additionally, she was unable to access the refrigerator door or the front or back doors of the house. Michelle used her wheelchair to travel between the locations where she had to work as a diabetes educator because they were all close by. However, whenever she dropped her purse or cell phone on the ground while traveling between locations, she had to wait up to 45 minutes before someone could assist her in picking them up.

Michelle was also unable to reach crosswalk buttons to activate them. She had to factor in two hours for a thirty-minute trip, just in case. Michelle's anxiety and depression worsened as she went out less frequently and grew more fearful of leaving her house alone because of the many things that could go wrong.

At that point, Rumba the puppy, entered her life and completely changed everything.

She applied for a service dog after a year of being quadriplegic and was given Rumba, a Canine Companion service dog, who had been trained for two years (since he was a two-month-old puppy) and knew and could obey 40 instructions.

With Rumba and Michelle, it was love at first sight, and Rumba quickly became Michelle's best friend and constant supporter.

Anxiety and depression in Michelle subsided right away. With the assistance of her best friend, Michelle was no longer on her own. Rumba was able to open the front and back doors, and the refrigerator door, bringing the food Michelle needed to her. Furthermore, she picked up any items Michelle dropped and put them on her lap. Rumba was also able to press the buttons to activate the crosswalk at crossings.

Although Michelle's mind often raced at 100 miles per hour, having Rumba by her side allowed her to calm down, smile, and savor the moment.

Rumba was diagnosed with a tumor in her abdomen at the age of 11 and sadly passed away in October 2022. Michelle didn't want to replace Rumba at first, but she noticed that she began to feel anxious and depressed again and was going out less often out of fear of becoming stuck on the road without assistance.

On February 10, 2023, Michelle adopted Earlene, a 2-year-old female yellow labrador-golden retriever mix who had just completed service dog training, from Canine Companion.

Earlene, who has a different temperament from Rumba, is showing Michelle how to connect with her. Michelle's depression and anxiety are at their lowest right now because Earlene is so tender, kind, and affectionate; she enjoys hugs; and she loves to help.

If you or a loved one struggles with anxiety or depression, consider getting a pet, especially a dog. Just like Rumba and Earlene changed Michelle's life, a pet can do the same for you (Gilbert, 2023).

However, it is important to note that while our pets have an incredible ability to lift our spirits, in many cases they do not act as a cure for these conditions, as it will depend on the level of symptoms. If you or someone you know is anxious or depressed, it is recommended that you first consult with your doctor so that he or she can recommend the best course of action in terms of treatment alternatives and possible medication.

People have always been interested in and connected to nature, interacting with and eventually developing bonds with the local wildlife. Early interactions between people and animals were primarily practical, but with time, companionship became a more important function for animals. Diverse opportunities for human-animal connection led to stronger bonds between people and animals, satisfying human aspirations to connect with animals on a deeper level.

Science highlights the psychological, physical, and physiological aspects of the human-animal bond, enhancing and promoting positive health outcomes. Numerous and obvious advantages of the human-animal bond to our pets emerge. We care about them, so we make sure they have access to food, shelter, healthcare, entertainment, and love.

But, as beautiful and fulfilling as this type of devotion can be, the pain of losing a pet is unthinkable. In the next chapter, we'll talk about different types of pet loss and look at suggestions on how you can learn to cope with them.

2

The Types of Pet Loss and the Grief They May Cause

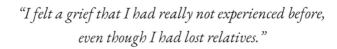

"I felt a grief that I had really not experienced before, even though I had lost relatives."

—John Grogan

We all know how devastating it can be to lose a cherished pet, and how it may leave us feeling hopeless and depressed. We genuinely loved them, and now we must go through the grieving process without our dearest friend at our sides. It may be difficult at first to imagine that you will ever be able to smile, laugh, or simply enjoy life again, but healing is possible, even if it may take some time.

I want you to know that my deepest condolences go out to everyone who has lost a dear pet. I want to assist you in taking the first steps toward healing. My goal is to offer empathetic, understanding emotional support to people who are preparing for or going through the loss of a cherished pet.

In this chapter, we'll talk about different types of pet loss, the associated grief, and what you can do to begin your journey to find healing.

NATURAL CAUSES

Even while losing a pet can be devastating for everyone, it can be especially tough to deal with sudden, unexpected pet deaths. A tragic loss like an unexpected fatal stroke or seizure can be harder to accept. Grief is frequently described as a period of closure, yet it can be incredibly difficult to achieve peace when a death occurs suddenly and under traumatic circumstances.

You can feel that life is incredibly unfair when you unexpectedly lose a pet. There is a feeling that your companion's life was unfairly terminated, leaving them with a life that was only partially lived and that completely vanished in an instant. These thoughts and emotions are very normal and understandable.

Pet owners who lose a pet suddenly and unexpectedly may experience physical and psychological shock. You might be shivering, having palpitations, headaches, stomach aches, insomnia, and other symptoms if you've recently experienced a bereavement.

Post-traumatic stress disorder (PTSD), which is characterized by recurring memories and a heightened state of arousal that persists for more than a month after a traumatic event, may even manifest in certain individuals. To experience this kind of trauma, you don't even need to have seen your pet pass away. It can be just as painful even when you weren't there.

Even if you don't have any signs of shock, you can discover that you're having recurring thoughts, a loss of appetite, guilt, rage, and grief, and that it's getting harder to function. Again, these emotions are normal.

You might think there was more you could have done to prevent such a sudden, tragic death. Furthermore, missing the opportunity to say goodbye is heartbreaking.

Coping With the Death of Your Pet

Here are a few exercises you might consider if you're having trouble with thoughts and emotions as mentioned above.

Understand the Incident

Tragically, unforeseen illnesses can occur. Just like us, animals can pass away before their time. Both guilt and blame involve attempting to comprehend what occurred and why. If you find yourself thinking the same thing over and over, try breaking down the circumstances that led to your pet's death. The goal is to understand your position in the event within a wider context.

For example, if your pet passed away due to a stroke, ask yourself these questions:

- Did you do anything that could have caused the stroke?
- Were you able to prevent the stroke from happening?
- Could you control the level of the stroke?
- Did you have any control over the impact of the stroke on your pet?
- Did you intend to harm your pet?
- Are you able to see everything that happens in the future?

The majority of the time, your response to these questions would be "no." You would have done so if you had the power to change what took place. Be kind to yourself and keep in mind that you did not intend on hurting your pet. You loved them and they had a wonderful life with you.

Consider Their Quality of Life

It's essential to consider your motivation. You went beyond what was necessary to improve your pet's quality of life. Keeping a pet enclosed in a padded chamber far from any risk is the only method to completely safeguard it from external harm. But would that improve their life's quality in any way?

Internal harms like heart disease, cancer, or epilepsy are out of our control. Nothing can shield a pet from these unexpected dangers.

Animals don't measure time the same way that people do, and they don't fret about the future or their mortality. Instead, they focus on the now. Your beloved pet lived a beautiful life with you. Perhaps the quality of a life, rather than its quantity, is what matters most, won't you agree?

Celebrate Your Pet's Life

Writing a letter to your pet and telling them about the life you had envisioned for them is one technique that can help with grief. Even if you only spent a brief amount of time together, you could write about the meaningful moments you shared and the significant impact they had on your life.

The most important thing is to honor the life your pet lived and their own character. Tell the story of the pet who liked having their belly tickled, had a favorite toy, or made people laugh with their amusing quirks rather than letting it be about "the animal that died a tragic death."

EUTHANASIA

Preparing for each stage of a pet's life is part of pet care. We frequently discuss the early phases, the difficulties of nurturing a puppy, or instilling good behaviors in them. Pet owners might not be as prepared for the difficulties that come with caring for an ill or elderly pet, such as determining when to bid them a final farewell.

For pet parents, deciding when to put a pet to sleep can be quite challenging. When various methods of reducing suffering and pain are no longer effective, a veterinarian may advise euthanasia, which is a gentle way of ending life. When you least anticipate it, such as when your pet has a terminal illness or has been in a disabling accident, euthanasia may be advised.

Experiencing Pet Loss After Euthanasia

Some people feel deeply at peace after choosing to euthanize their pet as a final act of kindness. When a pet has been seriously injured or is very ill, we commonly refer to putting them "out of their misery." However, for some people, euthanasia can bring up a wide range of challenging thoughts and emotions that are profoundly upsetting. Following euthanasia, typical responses include:

- Recurrent images of the pet being anxious and afraid at the end.

- Fear that perhaps there was another, untried route of treatment that was missed.

- The belief that it was either too early or too late.

- Feelings of guilt that include ideas like "I shouldn't have given up," "I should have realized something was wrong sooner," or "I should have sought out more opinions."

- Fear that their faith in us had been betrayed as they actually wished to live.

People often worry that their pet may still be alive if they had taken a different action. It can be challenging to consider the benefits of euthanasia with objectivity when one is experiencing the anguish and confusion of grief.

Many people profess to have repeatedly replayed their pet's death in their minds. This can be persistent at first or even for some time after. They may be concerned that they won't ever be able to remember the great times again. Although every individual is unique, many of us exhibit emotional or behavioral reactions when putting a pet to sleep.

Denial, bewilderment, astonishment, disbelief, rage, and sorrow are among additional emotions you could experience. A common reaction is that one feels as though one is "going crazy" or that one will never be the same again. It's also common to think about all the missed opportunities to spend time with your pet.

Some people may have a sense of disconnection after their pet has passed away as they discover that the world has moved on without them. With euthanasia, this can be even more pronounced.

Our behavior can be impacted by grief. Some pet owners discover that they are unable to move their pet's belongings—water bowls are left to evaporate, beds remain covered with tangled blankets from previous sleep, and toys are left lying around the house—while others pack everything away right away because they feel they cannot bear the constant reminders of their loved one.

As it is such a delicate subject, the entire next chapter has been dedicated to euthanasia, with suggestions that can help you cope with the loss.

OTHER PET LOSSES YOU MAY EXPERIENCE

Pet loss is not always about a pet passing away. Losing a pet due to being forced or obligated to give them up, when they go missing, or when they run away is also traumatizing. We'll explore this type of pet loss in this section.

Giving up a Pet

The tragic loss of a pet after a natural disaster, such as a hurricane or tornado, is a well-known type of pet loss. Many pet owners are compelled to leave their animals behind during natural disasters in order to flee the impending crisis or lose them during the evacuation process. Even after taking into account the trauma of being forced to leave their homes, losing pets during Hurricane Katrina was linked to an increase in psychosis. Forced abandonment was another aspect of the trauma of losing a pet during Hurricane Katrina. Forced pet abandonment during an evacuation exacerbates the trauma already experienced and raises the possibility of developing post-traumatic stress disorder.

People also have to give up their pets when they are forced to move to a location that doesn't allow pets. They tend to put a great deal of blame on themselves during this type of grieving process.

A Lost or Missing Pet

The loss of a pet can be upsetting, especially in terrible situations such as when a pet disappears or the pet parent has to give their pet up. The question, "What did I or did I not do that could have prevented the loss of my pet?" can cause a great deal of guilt and can exacerbate the confusion caused by the grieving process. The dilemma of disrupted grieving might develop when a pet goes missing. How long should it take a pet owner to conclude that their beloved animal must be dead? Is it preferable to wish the animal was still alive and living with someone else, or does this increase your concern that they will be mistreated or harmed there?

Coping With a Runaway or Lost Pet

For a variety of reasons, uncertain grief brought on by a lost pet can be very upsetting. Since the loss usually happens suddenly and unexpectedly, there is mostly no chance to say goodbye. This kind of loss might not be openly acknowledged by others. The loss is unclear because the pet may still be alive even though it isn't physically present. Even if this might be the case, it's important to remember that there has still been a loss and the link with the pet has been broken.

If one of your pets is lost or ran away, you would want to spring into action, right? Perhaps you feel so frazzled that you know what needs to be done, but don't know how. These tips may help.

- Call the animal control office in your area.
- Speak to nearby animal shelters.
- Start raising awareness locally.
- Begin searching.

- Don't forget to pay attention to other family pets.
- Find out what can be done to stop a similar loss from happening again.
- Find a trustworthy and understanding person to talk to.

A KILLED ANIMAL

Having a pet that has been intentionally or accidentally killed might prolong grief. A person may suffer disbelief, shock, sadness, anger, and guilt after experiencing this kind of abrupt death, which is particularly tough. You can experience flashbacks, nightmares, and other post-traumatic stress disorder symptoms if the death was awful. You can go through complicated mourning if you've had unsolved losses in the past or if you've struggled with anxiety or depression. When faced with all of these situations, one can really benefit from psychotherapy.

Even when we did everything in our power to ensure our pets' survival, it is a natural reaction to feel sorrow and try to understand why an animal passed away. Sometimes, however, we decide to place the blame on ourselves. Eventually, most people conclude that they played a very positive role in their pet's existence and that the death of their pet was ultimately beyond their control.

Guilt can (but need not) be crippling in situations where a pet passed as a consequence of an accident in which a person who cared for them was directly involved. That person *can* still find healing, though.

Coping With the Wrongful Death

Nothing can bring back a beloved companion animal who was unjustly killed, but we can take action to stop this from happening to other animals.

Peta offers advice on what to do in the case that a pet is purposefully killed as well as how to prevent it from happening (If Your Animal Companion is Shot or Poisoned, 2003).

The First Step

Immediately take your animal buddy to a veterinarian for care if you believe that they have been harmed. In the event that the animal passes away, have the body necropsied and obtain a statement from your veterinarian outlining the animal's condition or injury and the care given. Have lab tests performed to identify the poison's source if your companion has been poisoned, and then retain the test results for your records.

File a Small Claims Suit

You can file a small claims lawsuit without an attorney at your local courthouse if you know who caused harm to your animal companion. The health or life of an animal cannot be measured in dollars, but this straightforward legal action might disturb the offender enough to deter them from committing a similar offense in the future. You will be granted a court date after filing the form. Bring all of your veterinary bills, proof of any associated costs, and the veterinarian's signed statement to the hearing. A small claims court can only recoup the "dollar value" of the animal and your costs because animals are still sometimes treated as valuable property.

But you could also be able to press charges in a court of law. Find out who in your town, county, or state is in charge of looking into and enforcing the anti-cruelty laws, and then send that person or organization a brief, factual written statement describing the occurrence, including dates and approximations of times. Gather concise and factual written statements from witnesses, and if necessary, compose your own. Make a complaint to the police, the county or district attorney, or a humane officer.

Other crimes, including those against using a gun inside city borders and destroying property, may have also been broken in addition to the anti-cruelty legislation.

Reforming Local Laws

Working to change local animal-related regulations is another way you can support the protection of animal companions. It could be conceivable to create an amendment to an existing ordinance that, for instance, would require the town to hire a trained animal-control/humane officer. By proposing and supporting the improvement of existing legislation, you could try to attract the interest of local or county officials.

Never undervalue the local media's interest in accounts about animal cruelty. A well-documented case (with pictures, if possible) should be brought to the offices of your local newspapers and television stations in an effort to pique the curiosity of reporters.

Prevention

Keep your animal companions inside if you want to guarantee their protection. Free-roaming animals regularly face threats from disease, vehicles, other animals, and hurtful people, to name just a few. Many people think that cats and dogs are independent creatures who can take care of themselves, but if they are allowed outside, they need strict supervision much like kids do. Animal partners depend on their keepers' watchfulness to keep them secure.

Lex's
STORY

One month after she lost her childhood dog, Trey (who was a Jack Russel), Lex's friend picked up a stray dog whom she named *Chase*. This dog is a labrador retriever and pit bull mix who struggles with anger issues. Unfortunately, Chase displays signs of aggression toward other animals. Lex was advised to sign Chase up for dog training, which she did three times. However, the training did little to help him. Lex was faced with a dilemma—as she had run out of resources to help Chase with his problem, she had to consider giving him up for adoption.

Lex posted a very emotional video on YouTube explaining her situation, but also, how she worked toward processing the associated grief.

First of all, Lex feels that she took Chase in too soon after losing Trey. She didn't have enough time to process her grief after Trey's passing. But, because she was feeling depressed, she believed getting a new dog could change this.

It is clear that Lex loves Chase to bits, but understanding that she couldn't help him anymore, she decided to post an adoption opportunity online. Very soon after posting this, she received an email from a lady who was interested in adopting Chase. Let's call her "Linda." Because Lex was feeling too heartbroken, she ignored the email, trying to hold on to her dog for a while longer.

Lex suggests that if your dog is displaying some problems, consider sending them to training. She emphasizes that she didn't put Chase up for adoption because she doesn't care about him, but only because she couldn't afford to send him to training anymore.

As Lex included her cell phone number in her post, Linda sent her texts inquiring about Chase. When Lex informed her that Chase was still available for adoption, it made Linda very excited. It turned out that Linda is a professional dog trainer! Since they started exchanging messages, Lex sent Linda many pictures of Chase. Linda told Lex that she already bought many things to prepare for Chase's arrival, including a harness.

Lex dealt with the grief and guilt by reminding herself that she did Chase a kindness. She is grateful for the time she had with Chase. Knowing that he won't be going to a shelter, but rather to a professional trainer, provides her with a lot of comfort. Also, Lex's family and friends keep reminding her that she did everything she could and that she sacrificed everything to try and help Chase. Although these things are good to hear, Lex still admits that giving up Chase is one of the hardest things she ever had to do (Audacious Lex, 2018).

It's common to feel a sense of overwhelming loss and despair after losing a beloved pet. Grief over loss often feels unmanageable and can lead to a range of distressing and challenging feelings. You shouldn't ever feel guilty or ashamed about grieving over an animal companion, even though some others might not comprehend the intensity of your devotion to your pet. Even though everyone responds to loss differently, the extent of your grieving will typically depend on factors such as your age and personality, the age of your pet, and the circumstances of their passing.

Generally speaking, the more significant your pet is to you, the greater the emotional anguish you will go through. Even though losing a pet is an unavoidable part of pet ownership, there are healthy ways to cope with the pain and grief, and when the circumstances are perfect, you might even be able to open your heart to a new animal companion.

One way of losing a pet that proves most challenging is having to choose to have them euthanized. In the next Chapter, we'll talk about the process, how to know if it's time to say goodbye, and how to prepare yourself for this difficult choice.

3

Good Night, Buddy

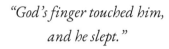

*"God's finger touched him,
and he slept."*

—Alfred, Lord Tennyson

The loss of a pet due to the sole instance of euthanasia may be the only grief that many individuals ever experience. Grief can become more difficult if a person feels guilty or unsure about their choice to put a beloved pet to sleep. For instance, research has indicated that arguments within families over whether it is (or was) appropriate to euthanize a pet can be exceptionally challenging (Ross and Baron-Sorensen, 2007). However, euthanasia also allows owners an opportunity to make final preparations for a cherished pet. There is an opportunity to say goodbye and arrange farewell gestures like a final meal, a night in, or a final goodbye as a way to show love and respect.

MAKING THE DECISION TO PUT A PET TO SLEEP

The fact that a pet's health deterioration is frequently unplanned makes end-of-life care difficult. Pet owners are often forced to make difficult decisions quickly while still experiencing panic and trauma. Sometimes, a major injury necessitates a quick decision, such as whether to undergo surgery or not, or whether to move forward with euthanasia.

Sometimes, a puzzling deterioration is followed by an abrupt diagnosis of cancer, kidney disease, heart failure, or another condition. Pet parents might have to decide between euthanasia, hospice care, or throwing everything at the issue during this crisis. Every decision has its own drawbacks. And in the midst of the chaos, pet owners occasionally make bad decisions that are tinged with remorse.

With that being said, how does one know when it is time to consider euthanasia? First, we must evaluate our pet's quality of life.

Pets' Symptoms That Indicate a Bad Quality of Life

Consult with your vet. They are the most qualified to support you as you go through this challenging procedure. Your veterinarian might be able to tell you with certainty in some circumstances when it's time to put your pet to sleep, but in other situations, you might have to make the final decision based on your observations of your pet's behavior and attitude. Here are some indicators that your pet may be in pain or no longer have a good quality of life:

- They consistently cough or breathe laboriously.

- They routinely soil themselves because of their extreme incontinence.

- If your pet is in pain, your veterinarian can help you assess whether it is chronic pain that cannot be managed with medication.

- They are unable to stand up on their own or trip over when attempting to walk.

- They aren't eating anymore or won't eat until you force-feed them.

- All or most of their favorite activities, such as taking walks, playing with toys or other pets, enjoying treats, or wanting attention and patting from family members, have become uninteresting to them.

- They frequently vomit or have diarrhea, which can lead to severe weight loss or dehydration.

While some pets pass away in the comfort of their own homes due to old age, many others suffer from serious illnesses, injuries, or have their quality of life significantly reduced as they age. In certain cases, it could be important for you to think about euthanizing your pet to save them from suffering.

When Is the Right Time to Say Goodbye?

You are in charge of your pet's care and well-being since you have a special bond with them. Many pet owners eventually have to decide whether their pets are going to live or pass away. The welfare of the animal and your family could compel you to make this choice.

Choosing whether to put your pet to sleep can be one of the hardest decisions you ever have to make. Although your choice is personal, it need not be made alone. You can get help and support from your family, friends, and veterinarian. Take into account what is best for you and your family as well as what is best for your pet. Life quality is vital for people as well as pets.

You may need to think about euthanasia if your pet can no longer engage in the activities that they once enjoyed with you and your family, if your pet is unable to respond to you in the typical ways, or if your pet is experiencing more suffering than joy. Euthanasia may also be a viable option if your pet is terminally sick or severely injured, or if the financial or emotional cost of treatment is exceeding your capability.

Your veterinarian can inspect and assess your pet's health, predict your pet's prospects of recovery, and talk to you about any potential limitations and long-term issues as they are familiar with pet attachment. They can describe the available medical options and potential results. You must comprehend your pet's condition because your veterinarian cannot decide whether to put your pet down. Ask to have the diagnosis or the implications for your pet's future explained again if there is any portion of it you don't understand. Normally, you will have time to process the information before making a choice.

HOW TO PREPARE YOURSELF

Discuss the matter with your veterinarian and ask any questions you may have if you decide that it is best for you to say a final goodnight. You must decide without any hesitation. However, it's equally crucial that you make decisions based on your pet's needs rather than your own.

Preparing for Goodbye

Knowing that euthanizing your pet is the kindest thing you can do, doesn't make it any easier. You will still struggle with a myriad of emotions, most of them not so good. Remember that this is completely normal and nothing to be embarrassed about. Love as pure as that between a pet and their human parent can never be embarrassing.

Pay the Bill Beforehand

Most veterinarians will ask you to take care of payment in advance, ensuring that you won't be concerned about a bill once everything is over. You'll be overcome with emotions—having to deal with a bill afterward will not do your heart any good.

Your Pet's Remains

You can work out a plan for what to do with your pet's remains with your veterinarian. Typically, you have two options: burial or cremation.

Take Time to Say a Final Goodnight

Although some veterinarians will visit the pet's home, most will perform the treatment in the clinic. Ask your veterinarian whether they believe it needs to be done right away or if you can arrange it for a few days later. Spend this time with your pet and spoil them unabashedly. Give them an exquisite bite of food you normally wouldn't allow, such as steak for a dog, if they want it or would be able to enjoy it. Savor every moment with them.

Give your pet some time to say farewell. You can decide whether to step outside or stay in the room with your pet during the procedure. Know that even though everyone feels differently, this choice is yours alone.

Ask a Friend to Drive You

Plan for someone else to drive you if the procedure is performed in a clinic. No matter how resilient and well-prepared you are, the event may have a considerably more severe effect on you than you expect.

What Happens During Euthanasia?

Making the difficult decision to put a beloved pet to sleep can make you feel even more anxious. This is especially true if you have no idea what to expect from the euthanasia procedure. American Humane describes the process beautifully, giving us a clear picture of what to expect (Euthanasia: Making the Decision, 2016).

- In most cases, your veterinarian will go over the procedure with you before starting. Asking your veterinarian for further information or clarification, if necessary, should never be an issue.

- Larger dogs may be easier to handle on the floor than smaller or medium-sized pets, who are typically placed on a table for the procedure. Either way, ensure that your pet has a cozy blanket or bed to lay their heads on.

- A qualified veterinary technician will typically hold your pet during the procedure. They are qualified to hold your pet safely and effectively so that the procedure goes along swiftly and effectively. It's crucial to give the veterinarian and technician ample room to do their jobs if you intend to be there for the entire procedure. Your vet will likely show you where to stand so that your pet can see you and hear you when you speak.

- Your pet will be administered sodium pentobarbital, a quick-acting anesthetic that also gently stops the heartbeat. The appropriate dosage of the medication will be drawn into a syringe by your veterinarian, who will then inject it into a vein. The front leg tends to be used in dogs. Cats can use either the front or the back leg. Your pet won't feel any pain from the injection itself.

- Before administering the injection, veterinarians commonly insert an intravenous (IV) catheter in the pet's vein. The catheter will lessen the possibility of vein rupture during drug injection. The drug may flow out into the leg if the vein bursts, which would slow down its rate of action.

- Before administering sodium pentobarbital, your veterinarian can provide an injection of anesthesia or sedative to your pet. Most of the time, this is done to pets who aren't likely to remain still for the IV injection. Typically, a sedative or anesthetic injection is delivered into the muscle of the back leg, and becomes effective within five to ten minutes. Your pet will become very sleepy or unconscious, which will make it easier for the veterinarian to administer the IV injection.

- After receiving the sodium pentobarbital IV injection, your pet will become fully comatose within a few seconds and pass away within a few minutes or less.

- The veterinarian will use a stethoscope to determine whether your pet's heart has stopped.

- After passing away, your pet might display intermittent breathing and exhibit mild muscle twitching for a few minutes. Also, your pet may empty their bladder or bowels. These occurrences are typical and shouldn't raise any red flags.

- The vet will typically ask if you'd want to spend a few last moments alone with your pet after confirming that they've passed away.

How to Explain Animal Euthanasia to a Child

If you have kids, it might be particularly difficult to put the family pet to sleep. Many children's pets were their first friend. How do you explain to your children that it is time to say goodbye?

- If your kids want to keep something from your pet, let them. This may include their favorite toy or leash.

- Talk to your children about what you're going to do to make your pet's transition from this world easier.

- Be truthful with your kids.

- To ensure that your children's last recollections of your pet are happy ones, make some final moments with them.

- Inform them that your pet is suffering and no longer enjoying being alive.

- Allow your kids to indulge your pet by offering them their favorite treats and some final cuddles.

If you have more than one kid, talk to each one separately about euthanasia.

BURIAL AND CREMATION OPTIONS

Sadly, choosing to put your pet to sleep is not the last difficult choice you will have to make. Even after bidding your pet farewell, you'll need to decide what to do with their remains. Most veterinarians will let you choose whether to perform a cremation or take your pet home to be buried; pets have the same options as people.

There are some alternative options. If you choose to bury your pet, you can either do it at home or locate a pet cemetery, which may include a head-stone or mausoleum. If you opt for cremation, you can spread the ashes or keep them in an urn of your choice. Blown glass that contains your pet's ashes is another popular option.

Douglas'

STORY

Douglas is a veterinarian at the Animal Medical Center in New York. Being a vet, he had to deal with euthanasia often. He would always comfort people by saying, "I understand what you are going through." But even though he thought he understood, he truly didn't, as he didn't experience something similar himself. Not yet, at least.

While he and his now wife, Eileen, were in college, they found a puppy in an Igloo Cooler box. His dad was a yellow labrador and his mother was a border collie. Her owners couldn't wait to get rid of her pups, so they placed them in the cooler box and dumped them next to the street so anyone who passed by and wanted them, could take them.

Douglas and Eileen named him Rufus. Although he wasn't Douglas' dream dog, he was more than Douglas could have ever imagined. He was with them when Douglas proposed to Eileen, moved with them to Columbus, Ohio, and then to Manhattan for Douglas' internship.

Rufus loved frisbees and swimming. If allowed to, he would swim day and night. He was quite special.

One day, Douglas received a phone call from his wife while he was at work. She informed Douglas that Rufus, who was now 15 years old, didn't want to eat. He told her to bring Rufus to the clinic immediately. Once they arrived, Douglas said that he didn't want to examine Rufus, leaving it in the hands of the other vets.

When Douglas was met by the radiologist, he said that he hoped to get the CT scans the same day. The radiologist then said, "Buddy, I'm sorry. He has metastasis." Douglas felt paralyzed, but knew he had to pull himself together—he had to tell his wife and daughter. He knew what he told other pet owners when scans came back like this: "On average, less than a month."

After he spoke to his wife and daughter, all three of them dropped to the floor, sobbing and hugging Rufus. After doing more scans, they discovered that Rufus had a splenic tumor and the tumor had spread to his lungs. An operation was not an option.

Thoughts ran through his head: "How is this even possible? Who am I as a veterinarian? I was unable to even help my own dog." But he was aware that death would inevitably occur despite their best efforts.

He heard the words replaying in his head, "You should take your dog home and spend some quality time with him," recalling all the times he advised owners to "spoil" their pets. After leaving the hospital, Douglas considered what Rufus would want. "If he is going down, he will do so with a smile on his face," he thought to himself.

They brought him to his favorite location, a bike path that encircled a sizable duck pond. He returned the sticks they threw with a smile and an expression of unbridled excitement as if to say, "What a wonderful day." The Frisbees were flying. Rufus sprinted back and forth hunting each one down but never truly returning it to them, definitely slower than in his glory days. "Typical," said Douglas.

As they completed a lap around the duck pond, they debated whether it would be better to let him leave on top rather than wait till this disease eventually took him out. After much discussion, they decided that they would have to put him to sleep since they didn't want him to ever experience agony. The world's most selfless beings, according to Douglas, are our pets, and it is our responsibility to be unselfish for them when they need it. They walked on while sobbing as they had made this difficult choice.

The following day, they entered the hospital quietly and had a colleague put him to sleep as Eileen and Douglas embraced him. He looked at them as he dozed off, seemingly asking, "What's wrong, guys? I am here for you." Douglas thought, "No Buddy, this time we're here for *you*."

Douglas remembers Rufus every day. His dog tag is permanently fastened to Douglas' key chain as a daily reminder to uphold half the moral standards that Rufus did. His memory is still very much alive. Every time he needs to deliver bad news or administer euthanasia, those two days are there with him. Now when he says, "I understand," he truly does (Palma, 2014).

Saying farewell is an essential step in managing the common and healthy emotions of sadness, grief, and a sense of loss. It makes sense that since your pet has a big impact on your life, you would feel as though you were losing a friend. After deciding to put your pet to sleep, you may want to say goodbye to them with the rest of your family. Spending the final night of your pet's life with them at home or paying them a visit at the hospital may be ideal. It's never easy to say goodbye. You'll need the support of your friends, family, and veterinarian.

While euthanasia can cause a great sense of agony, any type of pet loss can cause immense heartache. In the next chapter, we'll cover why it hurts so much and how you can navigate the pain toward healing.

4

The Heartache of Losing a Pet

"When you are sorrowful look again in your heart,
and you shall see that in truth you are weeping for
that which has been your delight."

—Khalil Gibran

For many people, losing a pet is practically identical to losing a loved one in every way. Yet, our culture hardly has any coping mechanisms. When a person passes away, there are eulogies, obituaries, religious services, and gatherings of family and friends. Additionally, we receive leave from work, and some companies even provide mourning compensation. We are encouraged to express our feelings and mourn in a variety of ways when a human passes away.

We generally don't have access to any of these customs or sympathetic people when a pet passes away. Most people are expected to immediately resume all of their daily obligations with little to no closure. The house is oddly quiet and full of bittersweet memories. The magnitude of our loss of a close friend and loyal companion is rarely acknowledged, simply because it was an animal.

It is common to make pet owners feel as though their grief is exaggerated, dramatic, or even embarrassing. Really, "it was just a pet." It is commonly underappreciated how strong of a link we have with our pets. We receive consistently positive feedback from our pets. We are loved just for being "us." They improve our mood and lower blood pressure. When that is lost, how could we not feel devastated? Only someone who has never loved a pet wouldn't understand that it's about a lot more than "losing a pet that we'll miss and grief."

WHY LOSING A PET HURTS SO MUCH

Many of us have close bonds with and deep affection for our animal companions. For us, having a pet enriches our life with companionship, fun, and happiness. They give the day structure, keep us socially engaged and busy, and even give us a feeling of meaning or purpose. They also assist us in coping with life's challenges and troubles. Therefore, it is normal to experience overwhelming sorrow and grief after the loss of a beloved pet.

Some people, such as those with severe disabilities, can lack the means to have a human companion. Or, after losing a loved one, some people have love to give, making a pet a good recipient. In such a situation, a pet can substitute a child, sibling, best friend, or lifetime companion.

Pets become a part of your family and way of life and soon pick up on your routines and habits. Furthermore, because we see ourselves in our beloved pets, humans project their thoughts, emotions, and ideas onto them. This means that losing a pet can be an extremely traumatic experience that leaves a great void in our hearts and lives, much like losing a close family member or friend.

The Magnitude of Pet Loss Grief

For most pet parents, a pet is a member of the family and is not merely "a pet." That is why having to say goodbye to them hurts so much. A lot of the same emotions that come with losing a friend or family member will likely surface with losing a pet. We go through the same stages of denial, anger, guilt, and depression before arriving at acceptance. It comes in waves. For those who have never owned pets, it may be difficult to understand the tremendous feelings felt when a pet passes away.

You shouldn't ever feel guilty or ashamed about grieving for an animal companion, even though some others might not comprehend the level of affection you had for your pet.

It takes a lot of getting used to living without our pet children, especially if they've been a part of our life for a while. For those of us who had pets growing up, they can seem to have existed forever. As a result, when they depart this world, a gaping hole is left in their place.

Because of the close bond we have with our pets, we can experience their passing as such a terrible loss.

A pet has a lot of unconditional affection to give, and that is at the core of everything. Cats are often stereotyped as being cold and calculating, but in reality, all animals are highly loving without the reciprocity or calculation that humans exhibit. In other words, a pet's affection is unwavering and without many of the games and complexities that characterize human relationships.

We can often get through the hardest days of our lives, thanks to our pets. For instance, cats often seem carefree. Cat owners will often say that if they're depressed, there's a good probability that one of their cats will come by and sit with them.

Because death isn't typically talked about at the dinner table, we're not necessarily equipped to deal with it, also making the loss of a pet feel more devastating.

Why Does It Feel So Much Worse Than I Expected?

We sometimes are oblivious to how much our pets affect our lives until they are gone. Only then do we feel the loss and emptiness that they once filled with unshakable joy and affection. It is only natural that we feel an acute sense of loss when our pets pass away because we have invested so much time and resources in developing special bonds with them.

To some people, their pet was their only companion who gave their life purpose. For example, some individuals (or couples) who cannot have children choose to adopt a pet to fill this void. This pet receives the same attention and devotion a child would have received, giving their *parents* a sense of purpose. When the pet passes, the loss felt is tremendous and similar to that of a parent losing a child.

For many, the passing of a pet is their first experience of loss. Many children grow up with pets, and since many animals have a far shorter lifespan than humans, they will eventually lose the companionship of this childhood pet. For some, the experience is simply worse than they expected as they've lost their closest friend.

Pets are often the only shield people have against loneliness, especially among the elderly. When their pet passes, the grief pours in with an overwhelming feeling of loneliness shortly after. While some may say, "Well, just get another pet," it's not that simple. True pet parents know that every pet has their own personality and way to show affection—aspects that will be missed and can never be replaced.

As we saw in the previous chapter, an undeniable cause of devastating grief is having to choose euthanasia. Not only does the passing leave an empty space where love once was, but this loss is often accompanied by guilt and remorse.

Everyone Grieves Differently

You go through the phases of grief in a different way than other individuals, and it can vary, even on a daily basis. Any of those phases—which we'll discuss in the following chapter—such as grief, denial, anger, bargaining, or any combination of them, cannot be approached consistently. Each person experiences these phases at their own particular pace and in their own specific style. They can also go back and forth between them. There is no linear phase.

We must acknowledge that we are experiencing these emotions and ensure that we find support and guidance to get through these various emotional domains.

Also bear in mind that the degree of your grief may differ depending on your age and personality, the age and personality of your pet, the circumstances of the animal's loss, and your relationship with them. People who live alone often have slower grieving since their companion played such a big part in their lives.

How to Navigate Grief Around Losing a Pet

Several things can be done to help you cope with losing your pet. These suggestions can be useful to you, but keep in mind that in the end, only you can decide what you need.

- Each person or family is free to choose whether or not to adopt a new pet. While some people decide to do this right away, others require some time to prepare their hearts for a new relationship.

- You could want to scatter your pet's cremated remains or bury their body in a meaningful location. A ceremony or ritual can be ideal to acknowledge how much your pet has meant to you.

- Taking care of yourself is essential while you're mourning. Try to exercise often and have well-balanced meals. Rest is vital, so if your sleep is being interrupted, try relaxing with a warm milky beverage or some calming music. Create new routines to replace the ones you already had with your pet, such as altering the time and place of walks. Avoid making any significant decisions and seek out relatives and friends who will be supportive.

- Try to talk about your feelings with a friend, family member, other pet owners, or the personnel at the veterinarian.

- Keep a memory box stocked with trinkets and your pet's beloved toys. Keep a record of special memories by keeping a scrapbook of pictures, painting a picture, or writing a poem or tale. A picture and a description can be posted on an animal memorial website.

- Allow yourself time to experience sadness, anger, guilt, or any other necessary emotions as you accept that the pain of this grieving is normal and something that should be felt.

HELPING A CHILD COPE WITH PET LOSS

It can be hard to inform children that a pet is gravely ill or has passed. They have a right to know what is going on and they too need time to grieve, even though we might want to protect them.

This may be their first encounter with death, and if it's handled properly, it can teach them important lessons about coping with loss in the future. Try to be truthful and use language that children will understand when sharing the bad news with them. Encourage them to keep in mind the enjoyable experiences you had with your pet and to document those memories in poems, drawings, or other creative forms.

Age-Appropriate Explanations and Activities for Kids

The emotional and cognitive maturity of a child determines whether or not they can comprehend what dying entails. Family Animal Services in Utah provides a general description of how children view death and dying.

Children Younger Than 2 Years Old

No matter what the cause, a child picks up on the tension felt by family members and reacts to a pet's death based on how those around them react.

Activity

Children don't all develop the same, but if the child is talkative and displays a degree of understanding, talk about the pet and their passing. Don't try and hide your emotions or say things like, "It will be alright." If your child cries, cry with them.

The 2- to 5-Year-Olds

The child may miss the animal as a playmate but not always as an object of affection. They'll view death as a transient condition, similar to how leaves fall from a tree in the fall and then reappear in the spring. However, as they become aware of the pain all around them, they could exhibit regressive behaviors (like thumb sucking).

Activity

Similar to the previous point, the passing of the pet must be discussed with the child. Ask them how they feel and don't downplay their emotions. Be honest with them and help them understand the truth of the situation, however painful. Children need to grieve too.

The 5- to 9-Year-Olds

The young kid may engage in "magical thinking," believing that death may be avoided or negotiated with, but they can start to see death as a permanent state. Children at this age start to notice a connection between their thoughts and their actions. For instance, a child might dislike caring for the animal and wish, albeit fleetingly, the pet would pass away. When the pet later passes away, the child can become hopelessly guilty.

Activity

If it was a situation where your child cared for a pet when the pet was unwell, talk about it with your child. Make every effort to reassure your child that the passing of the pet was inevitable, not their fault, and that they have nothing to feel guilty about.

Children 10 Years and Above

The child normally comprehends that death is final and that all living things eventually pass away. But comprehension and acceptance are not the same. The typical phases of grieving experienced by adults can also be experienced by the child, including denial, bargaining, anger, guilt, depression, and acceptance. They could also have further reactions:

- The child might relapse to outgrown behaviors like thumb-sucking or tantrums.

- The child might stop interacting with friends and family. They can struggle in school and appear uninterested in extracurricular activities.

- The child can fear being abandoned. They might conclude that as their pet could pass away, so could their parents.

- The subject of death and what transpires to the body can pique the child's curiosity. They might ask you awkward questions that are hard to explain.

Activity

If the child regresses to outgrown behaviors, don't reprimand them. Help them to open up about their feelings, reminding them that the phases they're going through are normal and nothing to be embarrassed about. You can also remind them that a pet's lifespan is far shorter than that of a human.

Furthermore, you can ask your local library or bookstore about children's books about death and dying. Don't simply hand the book to your child. Spend time with them, answering any questions they may have. If you're unsure about the answer, tell them that you'll work on finding an answer, and then do just that.

SUPPORTING A GRIEVING FAMILY MEMBER OR FRIEND

What do you say to console a friend or relative who has just lost a cherished pet? How can you be there for them by talking to them and offering support while they navigate their grief? Explore these suggestions on how to be more understanding and supportive of loved ones who are grieving the loss of their pet.

Share Any Fond Memories or Pictures You May Have of the Pet

If the grieving individual writes a passionate post about their loss, you can show your sympathies and compassion by respectfully commenting on a memory or an accompanying photo. They can find comfort in the idea that their pet had a positive effect on others in addition to being reminded of these wonderful moments.

If You Have Any Questions, Don't Hesitate to Ask Them

Do not press the grieving person if they are not providing many details. It's acceptable to ask them some questions or request more information if they're willing to talk and you're genuinely interested. While you don't want to pry, it could be beneficial to the mourning person to talk about their experiences and not keep them bottled up.

Use Their Pet's Name

Never call their animal companion "the dog" or "the cat." Even if you find it hard to comprehend how heartbroken someone would be over losing a pet, you should nonetheless be gracious. Use the name that has been given to them.

Listen More, Speak Less

If the person who is mourning wants to discuss it with you but you are at a loss for words, simply listen. You must keep your feelings to yourself, even if you don't understand or believe the individual is exaggerating the situation. You're there to offer assistance and support.

In addition, avoid talking about your own pet loss or how you would feel if your pet died because doing so may diminish their suffering and give the impression that you are competing with them in your grief. The best thing you can do is listen sympathetically since this is all about them.

Remind Them That Thanks to Them, Their Pet Had a Wonderful Life

Let the owner know they went above and beyond to ensure their pet was always pleased, whether it was purchasing the tastiest treats, the cutest toys, or sharing the trendiest pictures online.

Domesticated animals are entirely reliant on people for survival, which can add to our sense of guilt when they pass away. Could anything else be done? Should they have spent $7,000 on that expensive, potentially unsuccessful surgery? If the person had to put their pet to sleep for any reason, they might have second thoughts about it. Therefore, constantly emphasize to the owner what a lucky pet they were to have had such a wonderful pet parent.

Joyce's
STORY

Joyce felt that the loss of her beloved cat was sudden. Even though it was drawn out, her pet's passing was unexpected. Her grief was severe, and to an extent still is. She can't help feeling this way. A friend told Joyce that she needed to be gentle with herself. These words reassured her that she had the right to grief as she needed. She wasn't obligated to apologize for experiencing the grief, even after several months. When it comes to grief, there are no rules or time limits. She came to understand that grief doesn't always make sense, but comes in waves.

Sometimes, the grief would be expressed as uncontrollable sobbing, while at times she would just be silent with tears streaming down her face. Sometimes, she is able to talk about it without feeling the agonizing pain in her chest. But then, it appears again, suddenly. Still, she learned that all of this is acceptable and normal. She only needed to be gentle with herself.

Joyce learned that she shouldn't rush the grieving process. Also, she shouldn't ignore others who wanted to lend her an ear, or simply a shoulder to cry on. No one else had the relationship with her pet that she had, even if they, too, had a great love for their own pets. So, ultimately, the only thing that Joyce keeps in mind is that she must be herself, and keep showing herself kindness (Everplans Team, n.d.).

Our souls are deeply touched by pets. They teach us better ways to love ourselves and one another. They teach us how to love and embrace others unconditionally and accept them for who they are. Pets can provide some people with a sense of purpose in their lives because of their dependency, which can be a wonderful gift for those who are prone to depression or loneliness. Our most fundamental need for touch, affection, and physical contact is met by our pets.

Discussing the loss of a pet with others can be difficult because it can be a highly delicate and emotional issue. However, it's important to tell your loved ones about your loss because doing so can aid in your grief process and help you find comfort and support. Children may benefit from participating in age-appropriate grief rituals with you, such as sketching pictures of their pets, writing letters to them, or sharing happy memories of them.

Still, to effectively navigate our grief, we need to understand the grieving process. In the next chapter, we'll talk about the different stages of grief, what to do if you feel stuck, and what emotions to expect.

5

The Grieving Process

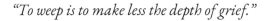

"To weep is to make less the depth of grief."

—William Shakespeare

Grief after losing a pet is a common and extremely personal reaction. Grieving for a deceased pet may be more difficult for some people than grieving for a deceased human loved one. One explanation is that there may be a lesser support system of sympathetic and understanding individuals. Everyone will be understanding if a person has lost a human loved one, including friends, family, coworkers, and others. They might offer food and company along with cards and flowers. When a pet dies, this is frequently not the case.

People will get together for a funeral or memorial service for the departed person to offer support to one another and a sense of closure. Again, this rarely happens when a pet passes away. Hurting remarks like, "You can get another pet," "Don't be so upset," and "It was only an animal," may exacerbate the sadness and sense of loneliness.

THE FIVE STAGES OF GRIEF

There are several stages to the grieving process, which can be quite complicated. Denial, bargaining, anger, sadness, and resolution are some of these stages. The stages may manifest as a complex series of emotions and feelings or in a recognizable order. Each stage's duration varies with the individual and usually across cultures. Some people might repeatedly go through a certain stage, like anger. Others may find resolve fairly quickly. In such a case, it is simply their particular response to their loss and doesn't imply that they loved their pet any less. The grieving process might last anywhere from a few months to a year in most cases, or sometimes even longer.

Let's examine these stages to expand our perspective.

Denial

Denial is a coping mechanism that helps us get past the initial wave of anguish and dulls the blow of loss. It's that painful period right after a pet passes away when you're sure you heard them "attacking" their favorite toy in the next room. You could also see them waiting by the door, asking to leave, or coming around the corner with their food bowl in their mouth. However, the figure at the door is a shoe, not your pet. It's not your pet that you hear, but your grief. It feels as though it has taken over every area your pet once occupied, including the void you feel in your soul. Denial is essential for enabling you to realize how deeply you loved your companion and how much you miss them. It is both perplexing and consoling.

Denial goes further than rejecting the loss. Sometimes it may seem overwhelming and bleak as if life's purpose was lost. Feelings of shock and numbness emerge because our bodies and minds only let in as much emotion as we can handle. As the shock wears off, suppressed emotions will begin to surface.

Responses and Symptoms

- irritability
- restlessness
- exhaustion
- despair
- disturbed sleep cycles
- illogical thoughts
- an overwhelmed mental state.

Recovering From Denial

- Just like you would with any other loss in your life, be kind to yourself at this time as you allow the shock to subside.

- Keep in mind that it could take a few days or weeks before you truly comprehend what happened and a new, stronger feeling begins to wash over you.

Anger

Anger generally follows denial and appears after reality sets in. Anyone can become the target of a grieving person's rage, including family members, close friends, veterinarians, and even your beloved pet. Though we should know better cognitively, our emotions sometimes encourage us to place the blame elsewhere, even on ourselves. "The vet ought to have expected this and taken action. I ought to have had a second opinion. Why did my pet abandon me this way?"

This stage can be very difficult since it may be challenging to manage how strong the emotion is. Recognizing these feelings and learning healthy ways to express them is essential. As we begin to sense emotions again after a loss, anger could predominate other emotions. One may contend that the anger we feel after losing a pet is only another indication of how much we loved them.

Responses and Symptoms

- a sense of injustice in life or circumstances
- agitation and irritability
- lack of patience
- frustration
- feeling severely stressed.

Recovering From Anger

- No matter who you are upset with—God, yourself, or someone else— it's acceptable to be angry, but you should use prudence when venting.

- Although what you're feeling is normal, remember that it may not be based on reality.

- Intentionally hurting oneself or others is never acceptable.

Bargaining

Bargaining, often with a higher force, oneself, or even a departed pet, is a common strategy used by many people to cope with their feelings of vulnerability and helplessness. A sense of regret about what they did or did not do for their pet can occasionally be present during the negotiation. It frequently consists of a tangle of strong, perplexing feelings that are difficult to reconcile. You say to yourself, "If only I could take him for one more walk," "If only I could listen to her purr one more time," or "I'd give anything for just one more day. Anything!"

Numerous veterinarians have stated that they commonly witness pet owners going through this stage of grief in an attempt to make sense of their guilt and regret. It's crucial to remember that the grieving process usually includes the stage of bargaining, which is normal and healthy. This third stage of grieving is characterized by feelings of remorse and responsibility. This stage can be particularly difficult for pet owners who think they could have done anything different to prevent the loss of their pet. They can occasionally take solace in good memories.

Responses and Symptoms

- They believe a second veterinarian's opinion could have been helpful.

- They believe that in an effort to rescue their pet, they have subjected them to too many painful and unnecessary surgeries and procedures.

- They believe they never should have taken their pet off their leash.

- They believe there was more they could have done to protect their pet.

- They believe they shouldn't have allowed their pet outside that night.

- They may feel they waited too long or decided to euthanize too soon.

Recovering From Bargaining

- Stop blaming yourself. This is the best strategy for overcoming guilt.

- Talk about some of your deepest regrets and darkest thoughts with someone you can trust to get a fair perspective.

- If necessary, seek expert assistance.

Depression

Sometimes, depression is just another way to say despair. Grief in this situation can help us recognize the inevitable separation we must confront. Some people start to reach out to others while others withdraw into their own worlds. Both times, mourners require encouragement and tolerance. Sadness aids in recognizing your wounds, which is the first step toward recovery.

Bargaining is all about the past; depression is all about the present. It could seem that because death is permanent, the depressing thoughts would last forever. Although depression is usually viewed as a problem that has to be addressed in daily life, it is actually a critical component of the grieving process.

Responses and Symptoms

- persistent thoughts of the deceased
- hopelessness
- self-isolation
- lethargy
- immense sadness
- crying
- in severe situations, suicidal thoughts.

Recovering From Depression

- You must become willing to enter that state of utter vulnerability since you will eventually have to enter the place where you can most easily sense the presence of your beloved animal companion.

- Maintaining that connection is the cornerstone of recovery.

- Make the suffering and tragedy a part of who you are becoming by incorporating them into your life, personality, and spiritual outlook.

Acceptance

In some ways, this is the most difficult stage of the grieving process. Acceptance is not the same as forgetting or betraying someone. What it does entail is accepting both the tragic reality of your pet's passing and the lovely, sweet life it led. It entails accepting that life itself has an end, a reality that we all understand intellectually but frequently forget about emotionally. Acceptance also acknowledges that you cannot replace the pet you lost with another. At this point, remembering is more likely to make people smile than cry.

Even while we may not particularly like this new reality, we must accept it and learn to live with it. Acceptance is not the same thing as moving past a loss or signaling the end of the mourning process. True acceptance can happen, but only after grieving. Examples include making new acquaintances and forming relationships, addressing our own needs, or simply starting to live again.

MOVING FORWARD

People who are mourning tend to forget that grief is a process and that new coping mechanisms are developed during this process. Typically, the lost pet is never forgotten. Most people never "get over" the loss when a pet passes away. However, those who survive come to terms with their loss. Loss becomes less severe, and a survivor can resume their normal life. One discovers they are more able to eat and sleep. Pets can help people form new relationships. Sometimes, there will still be tears and sadness, but there will also be increased happiness and passion for life.

What if I'm Stuck in My Grief?

When you have prolonged grief disorder (PDG), formerly called complicated grief, you become "stuck" in your feelings of loss, and your life is profoundly affected in many ways. If you still have an intense sense of desire for your pet and are distracted with memories or thoughts of them long after the stages of the grieving process have passed, then it may be a sign that you need support. For at least a year or more following the passing, if these yearnings and distracting thoughts occur practically every day, you should speak with a qualified expert who can determine whether you may be suffering from PDG and offer advice on how to break free from the grief.

If you are experiencing suicidal ideas due to your grieving or feel stuck in your grief, grief counseling can be a great comfort. Grief counselors can help you find more effective coping strategies for your suicidality and distress, provide a safe space where you can express yourself without fear of judgment, and assist you in better comprehending your own grieving process.

You can also try the following to get unstuck:

- Respectfully recognize and acknowledge your loss.

- Prioritize taking care of yourself.

- Make a conscious decision that your inner voice and thoughts will be kind and that you will be gentle with yourself.

The Grieving Process Happens Only Gradually

People progress through each stage of the mourning process at varied rates, and there is no defined time frame for it. Grief symptoms usually go away after one to two years. This timeline varies for each person, though. A person's emotions also tend to change over time and arrive in waves rather than seeing a gradual drop in grief. After a long period, grieving reactions frequently recur in response to triggers like birthdays, noteworthy occasions, holidays, and songs.

Even if the suffering can subside with time, it's typical to feel emotionally attached to the deceased pet for a very long time. Grief cannot be forced or hurried forward in a "normal" manner. Some people commonly begin to feel better in a few weeks or months, however, for others, the grieving process lasts for years. No matter how much agony you are experiencing, it's important to treat yourself kindly and let things develop naturally.

THE COMMON EMOTIONS AFTER
THE PASSING OF A PET

Grieving is personal, it's different for every pet parent, and they might not feel all the emotions that go along with it. At this time, it's their journey, their tale, and their experience that matters, not anybody else's. They could discover that the stages of grief recur, and many pet owners would describe the mourning process as "being on an emotional roller coaster." Despite how alluring they may seem; alcohol and narcotics should not be used by pet owners who are mourning since these will not help them through the process and will rather make it worse.

The pet parent who goes through the phases of mourning experiences not only emotional reactions but also physical ones, which can include the following:

- your immune system is compromised, making you more prone to colds and flu-like symptoms

- feeling feverish or too cold

- headaches

- nausea

- feeling ill generally

- heartbeats will fluctuate between rapid and slower beats.

Some pet owners experience acute isolation and loneliness. Please don't worry or feel embarrassed; these emotions are perfectly natural. When you express your feelings, it's not an indication of weakness or that your emotions are out of control. You shouldn't feel guilty about it because all it indicates is that you are mourning the loss of an animal you loved.

Never Suppress or Ignore Your Suffering

In the long term, holding in your emotions can only make things worse. You must address your grief head-on if you want to recover. Be confident in expressing your feelings. You have lost someone extremely precious and close to you, thus it's appropriate to cry or feel upset. If some days are more challenging than others, try not to be too hard on yourself. There will be occasions when your grief is triggered. These could be locations you frequently visited, the day your pet was adopted, or their birthday. When you are ready, make these days a celebration of the unwavering love you two shared. Support from others will greatly help.

Talking about your emotions and your pet can be quite beneficial. Don't be reluctant to talk to your family and friends, especially if they are familiar with your pet. They can be a source of comfort. You can also discover that writing out your thoughts is soothing. It can be quite challenging when a pet is stolen or lost since there usually is no closure. Writing down your thoughts and what you would have said to your pet before they went away is one thing that you can do. This can help you heal from any kind of loss.

Susan's
STORY

When Susan lost her beautiful steed of 16 years to colic, she was in such a state of shock that she couldn't eat. Her horse's name was DC. After her beloved DC passed away, Susan wept for days and weeks. She recalls feeling as though a physical weight was on her body. A trigger could be as simple as thinking about him or gazing at an old photo. Then, she decided to stop feeling foolish for grieving over "just a horse," as he was more than simply an animal that she had owned for 16 years. He played many roles, including confidant, comic, and adventure buddy.

Speaking about triggers, she decided to stop riding because it was difficult for her to be around other horse-loving individuals. She essentially stopped riding for four years. Although Susan had every intention of going back to it, she lacked the courage. Her father went to the stables to get her bridle, saddle, and tack trunk, which contained all of her riding equipment. It spent a very, very long time in the garage.

Susan recalls the day they had to put DC to sleep. She confessed to her husband, "I don't know what I'm supposed to do right now." He advised her to leave the house and go to work because staying in would be useless. She cried for the majority of her hour-long trip to school. She recalls being relieved when she arrived there. It felt like play-acting. She kept it from her students and carried on with her day as usual. Her brain was occupied by the children, so it was unable to "go there," allowing her to take a break from her sorrow. Maintaining her regular schedule helped her.

Susan sat down to write and produced a thorough horse eulogy. Then, she forwarded it through email to her immediate family, close friends, and everyone else she knew from earlier days who was connected to DC. She got some of the most kind, uplifting feedback in response to her message. Knowing she wasn't the only one who cherished that horse made her feel better. She found some solace in adding bits of other people's sorrow to her own enormous pot. Susan then truly knew that she wasn't alone.

She also grappled with the guilt she felt for being so upset about losing a horse when other people had lost a spouse or child, a career, or their health. She considered all the hurting people in the world, including refugees, children working in factories, and individuals who were being persecuted for their religious beliefs, and she felt that her issue was insignificant in comparison to these larger issues.

Insisting that it's okay to mourn loss because it's a natural part of the human experience, a friend reassured her that it was good to feel and express her emotions.

She was aware that there are a variety of enjoyable pursuits available besides the world of horses. Before DC passed away, Susan had been a lindy hopper for a while, but without him, she was able to become more actively involved in dancing. She started going to swing dance courses and camps with her husband. She had a great time. Fun anyway, though not on the same level as riding, and never a replacement, but still, a fantastic workout!

She went to see her previous trainer, who also happens to be a close friend, a year or two later. Susan was sort of coerced into mounting one of her friend's horses. Susan was really anxious, but once she was riding in that borrowed saddle, wearing a borrowed helmet, and only wearing jeans—she felt at home. She thinks the brief trip helped her realize it was time to pick up her passion again. And she was thankful for that (Friedland, 2015).

Grief is a normal response to losing a person with whom we have shared a significant portion of our life. You can easily relate a pet's grief process to that of a person who has passed away. Each person deals with loss in a unique way. There is no right or incorrect response when it comes to how you ought to handle your emotions. Remorse is a common reaction to the loss of a furry friend and can elicit a range of emotions. Feeling like you could have done more or that you didn't effectively protect your pet from illness, harm, or death is common.

When you're overcome with remorse, it could be difficult to deal with the death of a pet. While all forms of mourning situations often include these stages, dealing with loss is a very personal process, and each person's time in each stage, the depth to which they go during each stage, or how they cope and move on from each stage, is completely unique to them.

Heartache is a very real and prominent part of the grieving process. Not only do you have to deal with each stage, but also with the pain that comes with the loss. In the next chapter, we'll cover how you can cope with the heartache and what you can do to move toward healing.

6

Dealing With
the Heartache

*"You gain strength, courage, and confidence by
every experience in which you really stop to look
fear in the face. You must do the thing which
you think you cannot do."*

—Eleanor Roosevelt

The majority of pet owners are aware that a pet is more than just an animal, even though we might avoid talking about pet bereavement publicly in polite society. They are also a cherished family member who provides a great deal of unrestricted love, affection, and solace. That's because, unlike other relationships, relationships with pets give a natural connection that doesn't require much thought or worry. It's that simple: You love them, and they love you. This degree of loyalty and trust can be found in very few human relationships.

COPING WITH THE LOSS OF A PET

Your general mental health and well-being can improve by getting a pet. You can also improve your mood and sense of social support by spending time with animals. Loneliness and social isolation can be reduced and eased by having a pet in your home. An animal is like an extended version of yourself. They often imitate you, sit on your lap, and follow you. A highly symbiotic relationship develops.

So, what do we do when they're no longer at the door to welcome us in? Let's look at some strategies you can use to get through your grief.

Acknowledge the Reality of the Death

Remind yourself that you don't need "permission" to experience the emotional grief brought on by your pet's passing. You *will* experience natural feelings such as grief, loss, and sadness. Grief is said to be "emotional suffering caused by death or bereavement" and involves a process that is required to start the healing process (Vasquez, 2022).

There is no formula, set beginning, or conclusion to this path leading to healing, and no two people grieve in the same manner. As previously stated, there is no set order in which the stages of grief should occur. We all experience them at various times, on different levels, in multiple orders, and occasionally not at all.

There may be times when the grief will seem like it will swallow you. Sometimes, when you least expect it, loving memories of your pet can make you cry. One of the most painful things you will ever have to do is say goodbye to your pet. You may get through your grief by acknowledging that your pet has passed away and that these emotions are normal during the healing process.

Recognize That Grief Factors Are Different for Everyone

There are different factors that influence how we grieve as we travel the path to healing. This implies that since each person's factors are unique, so are our grieving experiences. Let's examine these factors.

Causation or Situational Factors

In the context of the book, the situation is that a beloved pet passed away. But was it a sudden loss, perhaps brought on by an accident or a natural disaster? Did you experience "anticipatory grief" because you were fore-warned of the imminent loss? When someone experiences an unexpected loss, they could have a hard time embracing it and end up in denial.

The grieving process is significantly impacted by the reason for the loss. When a pet dies naturally, people may respond differently than when it dies due to an accident or a crime.

Personal Factors

The degree of resiliency, emotional control, the significance of the loss in the person's life, and the support they receive from family and friends at that time are all factors that affect grieving.

Cultural Factors

Grief is considered a private matter in several cultures. However, in some cultures, grief is shared and openly addressed with others. The grief process after losing a pet would be very different for people, depending on the culture.

NEVER ALLOW ANYONE TO DICTATE YOUR FEELINGS

Because not everyone has had a close relationship with a pet, some people in your life may make dismissive remarks like "It was only a dog" or "Just get a new cat." However, the loss can be just as difficult—if not more so—for people whose daily routines are tied to the care of a pet and those who count on their pet as a source of undiluted love.

Just be aware that not everybody in your life might be able to understand how intense your grief is. Other than the people who are familiar with your pet, it's difficult for anybody else to comprehend your relationship. Try not to get perturbed by other people's remarks. Your sorrow is quite valid.

Oh, and you shouldn't feel bad for keeping Bud's belongings (or for sleeping with his blanket). While some people find comfort in it, others don't want a continual reminder. You do you. It will set off an extreme reaction and hurt if you had a significant connection that you've suddenly lost. That's normal. Don't forget it.

CONNECT WITH OTHER PEOPLE WHO HAVE LOST PETS

Connecting with people who have also experienced pet loss could help you begin your recovery. These individuals might comprehend the grieving process and refrain from discounting your experience. Consider contacting a pet loss support hotline, support group, or relevant message board if you don't personally know someone. If feeling depressed interferes with your regular activities, a qualified counselor can support you and assist you in learning to cope.

RITUALS CAN HELP TO HEAL

Lighting a candle, framing a cherished photo, planting a tree or flowering plant as a living memorial, spreading cremated remains in a pet's favorite spot, or preserving the pet's collar, tags, and favorite toy in a special box are all examples of ways to honor a beloved pet. Some people opt to bury their animals in special cemeteries. A little amount of a pet's ashes can be stored in a specially-made necklace. Some companies even create a man-made jewel out of pet ashes.

Create a Legacy

Your pet's ashes can be kept in a decorated box or urn within your house, but you might find solace in scattering them in a location that your pet loved (such as a beach, the park, or your backyard). You can fashion a bracelet or necklace out of their pet tag, keep a photograph of them in your wallet, or set their image as your phone's background. Consider printing a few pictures of your beloved pet, framing them, and placing them throughout your house. Seeing their beaming faces regularly may help you feel at ease and bring comfort.

Or use a memory book service to produce a photo book. If you prefer the old-fashioned approach, you might even wish to make a tangible scrapbook containing photos, a tuft of hair, and a piece of their favorite chew toy. You can open the book whenever you miss them and reflect on the wonderful years you had with them.

Not everyone will be interested in this choice, but if it appeals to you, think about having a bespoke stuffed animal made to resemble your pet. If you want something comforting to hug while you're feeling down, this can be extremely useful.

Try to Maintain Your Normal Routine

Develop your own routines or modify the ones you had with your pet. You may try keeping up your habit of walking your dog every morning before work, but perhaps take a different route or focus more on your personal health and fitness. Sit in your emotions. You may think that the world expects you to get over your loss quickly and that you must "carry on as normal," even though it is your "normal" that has changed. In order to start establishing a new normal, you must allow yourself to experience your loss. Although the life you enjoyed with your animal companion is sadly over, it can and will be restored.

FOR SENIORS WHO ARE
MOURNING THE LOSS OF A PET

We go through an increasing number of significant life changes as we age and the passing of cherished friends, family members, and pets can be among them. Seniors who are retired may be more severely affected by the death of a pet than younger people, who may be able to seek solace from close relatives or redirect their attention to work. Your pet was likely your only friend if you are an older adult living alone, and caring for the animal gave you a feeling of routine and purpose.

It's acceptable to feel sad and grieve after losing a pet, but it's just as crucial to recognize continued depression's warning signals. Previously, taking care of a pet would have taken up a significant amount of your time and also improved your mood and outlook. When you're depressed, you could experience exhaustion, loneliness, and isolation.

- A change to your daily routine can be beneficial; try to fill your time with things you enjoy doing. Taking up a long-forgotten pastime, enrolling in classes, and helping friends, animal rescue organizations, or animal charities care for their animals can all be beneficial.

- Talk about your emotions with loved ones who understand how painful the loss is. Don't keep your sorrow to yourself; instead, reach out to a pet bereavement support line if talking to friends makes you uncomfortable.

- Regardless of whether you feel like talking to anyone, accept offers of assistance and support. You will find comfort and support from friends, family, and volunteers as you remember your pet with affection and work through your grief.

- Living without a pet can be difficult, especially if they gave you companionship and a feeling of purpose. One great way to assess your readiness to get a pet again is to volunteer to help animals in need.

- If you're not ready to adopt a new pet yet, don't allow anyone into forcing you to do so. You know your own heart best. Be assertive and firm when others try to force a new pet on you, especially if you're not ready.

PRACTICE MINDFUL GRIEVING

You can move through your grief with the aid of easy mindfulness activities rather than remaining stuck. Here are a few ideas you can give a try:

Mindful Breathing

You can perform this exercise anywhere, at any time.

The goal of mindful breathing is to help you focus on the present now, reconnect with your body, and allow thoughts to pass through your mind without becoming sucked into them.

You must use your diaphragm to breathe during this exercise, paying close attention to the rise and fall of your chest. Feel the warmth of your breath as it leaves your body by taking slow, deep breaths in through your nose and out through your mouth.

Rather than thinking about anything else, try to concentrate on counting your breaths. You'll have thoughts, and that's okay since you're not attempting to avoid them. Recognize any thoughts you have. Don't berate yourself for having sad, guilty, or angry thoughts. When you are mourning, these emotions are normal.

If you notice that your thoughts are drifting to your grief, focus on returning to your breath count and focusing on each count to try and control your thoughts. Keep in mind that if you regularly practice mindful breathing, it will become easier over time, helping you to maintain focus and keep moving toward healing. Consistency is the key to achieving the best results mindful practices have to offer.

Mindful Self-Compassion

It can be difficult to be kind to yourself while you're angry or feeling guilty, especially if you believe you played a part in your pet's passing. You can strive to cultivate self-compassion through this mindfulness activity. It's easy to become mired in a pattern of negative thoughts, a blame spiral, and loss-related emotions when you're mourning. Breaking the pattern and changing those challenging thoughts are the goals of this practice.

Change your self-talk by using succinct, kind, and meaningful statements. It could say, "May I find the courage to go on without you," "I am not my thoughts," or even "May I develop the self-love to forgive myself." It's a great idea to work this into your morning routine. Spend five minutes each morning speaking such positive affirmations.

A Mindful Visualization

Combining mindful breathing with the visualization exercise "Leaves on a stream" can be beneficial for some people.

Close your eyes and see a stream flowing through a forest as you focus on your breathing. The trees all around you are shedding their leaves. Grab a falling leaf and tie an emerging thought to it. Next, let the leaf gently fall into the stream and allow it to float away from you.

Anything counts, from your dinner plans for tonight to the way your pet passed. Acknowledge the thought, give it a name, and then allow it to drift away from you.

Abandon the Deadline

Many people have a timeline for when they should be done grieving. I've heard many people say, "It's been six months, I should be feeling better by now."

Try to visualize the date disappearing from a calendar each time this thought enters your mind to bring your attention back to the present. Concentrate on your breathing and what you can currently see, touch, hear, taste, and smell.

Grief has no set end date and does not go in a straight path. Rather, it resembles a roller coaster track with highs and lows that repeatedly go around the same loop.

STRETCHING FOR GRIEF

Your body can release the stress and pain of grieving with the correct kind of physical activity. Exercise will help you sleep better, stay mentally stable, and experience a greater sense of well-being, whether you go for a leisurely walk outside, do yoga for grief, or return to the gym. If you breathe and sip water as you work out, bonus points!

Professor Ueno's

STORY

For this chapter, I want to turn things around a bit. I want to tell you the remarkable true story of unwavering loyalty and pure love between a dog and his master.

This is the story of Hachiko.

Hachiko's owner, Eizaburo Ueno, a professor in the University of Tokyo's agriculture department, brought him to Tokyo in 1924. Throughout his owner's life, Hachiko said his goodbyes at the door and met him at the neighboring Shibuya Station at the end of the day. The two carried on as normal until Professor Ueno failed to board the expected train one evening in May 1925. At the university that day, the professor suffered a cerebral hemorrhage. Hachiko was waiting at the train station, unaware that his beloved owner had passed away.

After his owner passed away, Hachiko was taken in by the family's former gardener, but he frequently broke free and returned to his former residence. After some time passed, Hachiko reportedly recognized Professor Ueno was no longer living at that house. He then went to the train station, where he had previously been with his master numerous times, to look for him. Hachiko looked forward to Professor Ueno's arrival every day. But he failed to find his friend among the station's commuters every day.

Other passengers were drawn to Hachiko because of his constant presence at the train station. Hachiko and Professor Ueno were regularly noticed together by many of the people who frequented the Shibuya train station. The commuters were moved by this and brought Hachiko food and goodies.

Hachiko only showed up in the evening, right when the train was expected to arrive at the station, for the next decade.

One of Ueno's pupils noticed the dog at the station that year and discovered Hachiko's story. He visited the dog often and throughout the years wrote various stories about his extraordinary loyalty. One of these pieces, which appeared in a Tokyo newspaper in 1932, brought attention to the dog on a national scale. Hachiko became a household name. The Japanese people were moved by his devotion to his master's memory and saw it as an example of the kind of familial loyalty they should all strive for. Hachiko's vigil was presented as a model by parents and teachers for kids to follow. Over time, Hachiko's renown for faithfulness turned into a national emblem.

At Shibuya Station, a bronze statue was unveiled in April 1934, and Hachiko himself was there. The statue is still in place and is a very well-liked gathering place. Bronze paw prints and words in Japanese describing Hachiko's loyalty permanently commemorate the location where he waited for the train.

On March 8, 1935, Hachiko passed away peacefully and alone on the street close to the Shibuya Station.

At Tokyo's Shibuya railroad station, a solemn service of memory is held every year on April 8 to honor Hachiko's faithfulness. Numerous dog lovers gather to pay tribute to his memories and loyalty (Wulff Hauglann, 2021).

Losing a pet is heartbreaking. Spend some time discussing the situation with sympathetic friends and relatives. You should never be afraid of your feelings, nor should you allow them to humiliate or embarrass you. While it's common knowledge that crying promotes healing, it's acceptable to express your emotions in other ways as well. It's important to remember that sadness can pass and that there are techniques you can employ to help you come to terms with your loss.

There is no proper or improper way for someone to handle grief. Even while it can seem like you're taking a while to come to terms with the loss of your pet, it will get easier with time. It is crucial to be aware of how challenging dealing with a pet's passing may be. Give yourself enough time to grieve, and if you need help getting over something, talk to a loved one you can trust or a professional.

Because not all people—even some pet owners—are not animal lovers, some will not understand the pain and sorrow you experience after losing your beloved pet. Unfortunately, we can't always choose who we spend our days with, meaning you will likely come across people who lack the sympathy you need to process your loss.

In the next chapter, we'll talk about dealing with these situations and how to cope with disenfranchised grief.

May we all find love, respect, and loyalty as was witnessed between Hachiko and his beloved master.

Good Will

Helping others without expectation of anything in return has been proven to lead to increased happiness and satisfaction in life.

I would love to allow you to experience that feeling during your reading experience. All it takes is a few moments of your time to answer one simple question:

<u>Would you make a difference in the life of someone you've never met without spending any money or seeking recognition for your good will?</u> If so, now is the perfect time.

I humbly ask that you take a brief moment to leave an honest review of this book. It won't cost you anything but 30 seconds of your time—just a few seconds to share your thoughts with others.

Your voice can go a long way in helping someone else find the same comfort and solace that you do.

Simply scan the following QR code or enter the URL corresponding to your region in your favorite web browser:

US	UK	AUS	CA
review.headuppress.com	*review.headuppress.com*	*review.headuppress.com*	*review.headuppress.com*
/ppoth.us	*/ppoth.uk*	*/ppoth.aus*	*/ppoth.ca*

7

Sorry About Your Pet. So... What Are You Having for Dinner?

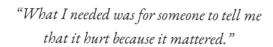

*"What I needed was for someone to tell me
that it hurt because it mattered."*

—John Green

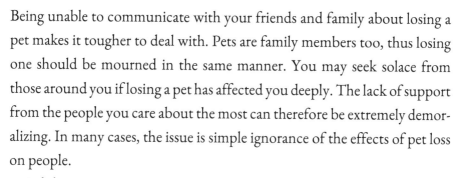

Being unable to communicate with your friends and family about losing a pet makes it tougher to deal with. Pets are family members too, thus losing one should be mourned in the same manner. You may seek solace from those around you if losing a pet has affected you deeply. The lack of support from the people you care about the most can therefore be extremely demoralizing. In many cases, the issue is simple ignorance of the effects of pet loss on people.

While some people may not cry or display any overt signs of upset, others may be very emotional. Do whatever you need to do to cope—there is no right or wrong way to grieve. Talk about your pet and the significance they had for you. Speaking about your feelings can be challenging, especially if those around you are not sympathetic. People frequently make the comparison between pet deaths and human deaths and conclude that a pet death should be less important; however, this can't be further from the truth. A pet's death can feel just as painful and emotional, especially if you were close to them.

WHEN FRIENDS AND FAMILY DO NOT UNDERSTAND

When a pet with whom you shared a deep relationship passes away, it can feel like you are missing a part of yourself. It can be a challenge to find someone who truly understands. The most ignorant things are often said by those closest to you. They attempt to put things into perspective by saying, "It was just a pet." When they suggest, "Get another one," they are attempting to be helpful. They don't realize that their comments are unkind because they reveal a lack of understanding of the magnitude of your bond with your friend.

How It Feels to Have a Loss Dismissed by Others

In general, ours is not a culture that is used to dealing with grief. Because of this discomfort, social norms that prioritize avoidance and promote a "stiff upper lip" among the grieving and a speedy return to daily activities following a loss are more common than those who view grief as a gradual process. These more general cultural inclinations frequently combine with the message that animal deaths are just not significant.

Unfortunately, some losses elicit more stigma than compassion. Responses from others could make you feel guilty or embarrassed rather than reassured. Grief typically progresses through a variety of stages. If you are unable to mourn openly, it may be difficult to go through these stages in a meaningful way.

Some People Find Loss and Grief Uncomfortable

Unlike in the past, when people saw life and death as two sides of the same coin, bereavement and death are now taboo topics in many contemporary societies. Death is a reality of life, although most of us would prefer to put off thinking about it until we are left with no other choice.

Furthermore, even though you currently have no option but to accept your loss, your larger network of supporters might decide to keep your grief at a distance. It's critical to realize that this isn't personal and doesn't represent how they feel about you or your pet. Instead, it could be that thinking about death, loss, and sadness makes people uncomfortable and makes them want to avoid having to deal with their own grief in the future.

They May Be at a Loss for Words

People often distance themselves from others who are mourning simply because they are unsure of what to say or are afraid of saying the wrong thing. Your friends or family might be reluctant to bring up your pet because they don't want to offend you or trigger painful memories.

They might not be aware of it, but you can't be reminded of your pet when you're already thinking about them constantly. People frequently don't realize how vital it is to talk about a lost loved one as a way to honor their memory and maintain the bond until they go through a time of grief themselves.

They Might Not Be Aware
That You Need Support

Most of us have a lot going on, both good and bad, only because life is hectic. Your friends and family may be too preoccupied with their own issues to realize that you need help. This is not to say that they don't care.

You might need to explicitly explain this to your loved ones and request their patience and support if you feel the need to talk about your pet loss pain. To assist in developing common expectations, it can be useful to specify precisely what you need.

In the End, It's Not Personal

The way most people behave, especially during your period of grief, is not necessarily aimed at causing you harm. Regardless of the circumstances, the loss you have endured and the anguish you are feeling are real. Never classify your sorrow or think about who has "the greatest right" to mourn. Grief is a unique and personal experience, and it is never fair to compare one's losses to those of others. Those who have never had pets find it challenging to comprehend the importance of having a bond with an animal. Although you are feeling a range of emotions right now, keep in mind that it's not your fault. Instead, attempt to constructively and positively express'to them why and how much your pet means to you. People who are close to you will pay attention.

Communicating With Extended Family and Friends About the Significance of the Pet's Loss

If you require help with funeral arrangements or simply someone to listen when you need to talk, don't be hesitant to let people know. Even your closest friends and family members sometimes struggle to know how to support you when you're grieving. Consider expanding your social network by making new friends if you don't feel like you have anyone you can ask for help during this tough period.

Let them know how much the pet meant to you and your family by being open and honest about your feelings. Sharing memorable experiences is one way to do this. They can be included in the planning of the funeral and memorial service. Never force your emotions on others; instead, speak and listen without bias.

TREATING AND COPING WITH DISENFRANCHISED GRIEF

The term "disenfranchised grief" refers to grief that isn't fully, or perhaps sometimes even partially, recognized by society. This category includes a variety of grieving situations, including losing a friend, miscarrying, placing a child for adoption, and losing an ex-spouse. Too frequently, the loss of a pet is experienced as disenfranchised grief.

You could feel that your grief is not being acknowledged as much as it would be if a human family member had passed away when you lost a beloved pet. Or, a loved one might be going through this secret grief right now if they recently lost a pet. This can be very distressing. When they need support to deal with their loss, many pet parents feel alone and unheard. The friendships you've formed around your departed pet can suffer a genuine and significant influence on your routines. The effects on your own life after the passing of a pet can be profound.

Pet owners may even have a sense of alienation from the animal-loving community. For instance, those who have experienced the terrible loss of a young pet may unwittingly minimize the suffering of losing an elderly animal by saying, "At least they had a long life. It was to be expected." Or people who love dogs and cats could find it difficult to comprehend someone who is mourning the loss of a little animal like a hamster, rabbit, cockatiel, or snake. The fact that everyone brings their own experiences to the table makes it a challenging environment to navigate.

Complications from disenfranchised grieving frequently occur that rarely happen during other, more socially acceptable phases of grief. Because you don't feel "allowed" to express your feelings around your loss, your depression or anger may get worse. You might not have gone through the customary mourning rites and ceremonies. Funerals are a milestone that is often skipped with animals, but they are an important part of the grief process for emotional reasons as well as the 'disposal,' to use a cruel term, of the body.

The purpose of our funeral rites and ceremonies is to recognize the value of the deceased's life. They serve as a means of saying farewell and keeping in mind the being who will no longer be physically present in our lives.

Naturally, this can't guarantee closure, but it's a way to show the world that the lost pet mattered. Also, it professes how important the pet's relationship with you was. Some people feel as though they must bid their companions a final farewell while alone, without the help of the larger community.

Knowing this, it makes sense why disenfranchised grief is sometimes called "paradoxical." The aforementioned problems make it worse while also diminishing it due to society.

How to Cope in Such a Situation

Find ways to communicate your sorrow: Many people find it beneficial to write about their pets, make picture books, sketch or paint, or create in some other way, even if they feel they can't express their loss to their larger network.

Remind yourself that you are entitled to grieve: It's okay to ask for time and space to mourn the loss of someone or something you love.

Reach out to your network of supporters: Your loved ones might not be aware of the extent of your current pain. Asking for help may lead you to someone in your circle who has also experienced the loss of a pet.

Recognize the sincerity, importance, and validity of your love for your departed pet: Your pet mattered to you, and your sadness is real.

Make up your own rituals: Pet parents now have the option to say good-bye to their pets and preserve sentimental items like paw prints or hair strands at a rising number of pet crematoriums. You could find it useful to establish your own rituals and memorials for your pet, with or without this option.

Understand that you are not alone: Some pet parents build websites in honor of their beloved pets. People often come forward on these sites and start talking about their own pet loss experiences to offer and receive comfort. This simply serves to prove that we pet lovers are not alone in our experience of love and loss. We belong to a community. On these websites and in private Facebook pet loss support groups, there are always people willing to listen.

How Can We Assist Others Who Are Grieving Without a Voice?

Describe their feelings: People who experience disenfranchised grief usually think that they are not permitted to communicate their feelings. Yet, one of the first steps to understanding emotions and coping with them is naming your feelings. It's vital to recognize that there are no good or bad feelings. Every feeling can be experienced during a loss, including shock, denial, anger, guilt, and anxiety, as well as sadness, relief, and release. There is no hierarchy in our emotions, and there are no good or bad ideas. It may be beneficial to someone you know to express their emotions following the loss of their pet.

Offer validation: This entails giving someone the message that their feelings matter. We don't have to feel the same way, but letting someone know that we recognize their suffering and recognize that they have lost someone extremely important to them may be incredibly helpful.

Respect the other person's loss: Regardless of the reason for a person's loss, it is not our place to determine whether or not their mourning is "real" or "appropriate." People experience their emotions. Though our emotions may not be the same, empathy enables us to perceive and comprehend when another person is in pain. Even if we have experienced a similar loss, we must be mindful of the fact that other people's grieving won't necessarily resemble our own.

Joe's

STORY

Nine months after Joe lost his dog, Gromit, he decided to sign up as a foster parent at a no-kill shelter. But then, he took in Red, a Doberman. Being a foster parent to a dog would mean that he would only have to take care of the dog temporarily. However, as Joe was sitting on his couch, Red walked up to him and put his head on Joe's lap. As Joe stroked his snout, he knew that he was going to adopt him.

Red was otherwise in good health when he first began wheezing. He was only seven years old. Joe was told by the veterinarian to go back if Red didn't feel better in a couple of weeks, only suspecting allergies. A chest X-ray two weeks later revealed a mild case of pneumonia, and the veterinarian sent them home with antibiotics in the hopes that Red would improve quickly. Joe gave him a pill at around 1:00 p.m. and left for work; but when he came back that night, Red had passed away.

Despite his best efforts, he can't seem to get rid of the image. Even though he lost both his father and sister, the loss of his dog felt worse. "How could the loss of a dog possibly hurt as much as the loss of a family member?" he wondered to himself. As the sorrow persisted, he tried to understand this as part of his grieving process.

Joe realized how powerful the animal-human bond is. He came

to understand that he had begun the grieving process feeling surprised and even ashamed that he was grieving his pet more than his sister and father. The couch never felt so lonely or the apartment so quiet during the months he resided there after Red passed away.

He understood that losing an animal might be particularly difficult because of the unconditional, nonjudgmental love that animals bring—they're just happy you're there. Living alone made losing his dogs more traumatic. Even though having a pet can help reduce loneliness, especially for single individuals, dealing with it when they pass away can be more difficult.

A few weeks after Red passed away, some dog park friends suggested hosting a gathering in his honor. Joe was appreciative of the gesture, but when he entered and exchanged hugs, he felt awkward as he took out the box containing Red's ashes and placed a recent photograph on the table. He had the impression that even those who had met just for this reason would prefer to utter a brief "I'm sorry; how are you doing?" rather than addressing the elephant in the room. They didn't start talking about Red until after a few hours and numerous drinks had passed.

His least favorite response was when well-intentioned people constantly asked him when he'd get another dog. This response almost seems to be saying, "Get over it already. He was only a dog." One is as good as another, right? Others appeared hesitant to express their sympathy for Joe, but he suspected that this was because they were trying to avoid facing the prospect of losing their own animals or are trying to forget the loss of a prior one. He is thankful, though, that many of his closest friends, relatives, and colleagues have developed amazing and sincere empathy.

Joe moved to his sister Rebekah's house in southern Maine two months after Red passed away to work on literary projects for a year. There, Maya, the lively chocolate 124abrador owned by his sister and brother-in-law, keeps him company and serves as a constant reminder that he will someday, most likely within a year, be prepared to adopt once more.

On a shelf in Joe's bedroom, Red's ashes are currently housed in a gorgeous wooden box that is displayed in front of a lovely drawing that a coworker's son made for Red after he passed away.

Gromit's ashes are buried in the woods behind Rebekah's house with a headstone that reads "Thank you." At the time this story was published, Joe was still working on the words that would go on Red's headstone (Yonan, 2012).

One aspect that might make grieving over the loss of a pet more difficult is the reality that not everyone understands it. Some individuals believe that mourning a pet is improper or that a pet's passing shouldn't be as painful as a human's. They might not understand because they don't own a pet or because they are unable to appreciate the companionship and affection that a pet can provide. One of the most difficult things about owning a pet is realizing that you have a higher likelihood of outliving it. On the bright side, it allows you to save and take care of a variety of creatures throughout your lifetime.

However, nothing can make the sadness of losing an animal you had been with every day for a long period any easier. Though losing a pet is terrible, having friends or family who don't understand the bond you share with your pet can make it worse. Despite their best efforts, there are times when misconceptions can make support appear to be lacking. The good news is that it's not too difficult to find alternative sources of support. Although it is hard to be unable to rely on the ones that we value most, there are other ways to take solace in dire situations.

Reaching out to those closest to you can be an important first step on the road to recovery. Even while some of your friends and relatives may feel awkward about your loss, some of them will want to be there for you. Talking about your thoughts and feelings won't make you a burden. Instead, it could aid them to comprehend the passing of your cherished pet and help everyone learn how to honor their memory.

Nonetheless, the grieving process can be a lonely experience at times and is a time when many people, unfortunately, neglect to take care of themselves. We will discuss self-care in the next chapter, why it is essential, and how you can keep on looking after yourself even in grief. Your pet would want you to be happy and well.

8

Self-Care During the Grieving Process

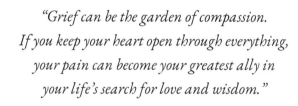

"Grief can be the garden of compassion.
If you keep your heart open through everything,
your pain can become your greatest ally in
your life's search for love and wisdom."

—Rumi

Because of how important our ties with our pets are to us, losing a pet can have a detrimental effect on our physical and emotional health. People who are grieving the loss of a pet can utilize a variety of coping mechanisms to get through the process while looking after their overall well-being.

LOOK AFTER YOURSELF

According to research, when we experience grief, our brains physically change (Silva et al., 2014). Our emotions and mental processes can be impacted by these changes. Many people experience feelings of sadness, anger, relief, depression, irritability, guilt, or loneliness as a result of grief. Some people who are grieving have mental symptoms such as bewilderment, difficulty concentrating, a persistent focus on their pet, or the perception that they can see or hear their pet. Some people may experience anxiety and depression after losing an animal companion.

Physical symptoms of grief from pet loss can include exhaustion, insomnia, tightness in the chest, a hollow feeling in the stomach, dry mouth, and aches and pains.

Self-Care Essentials

Since grieving the loss of our pet companions may be just as hard as grieving the loss of a family member or friend, if not more so, there are beneficial actions to take, as well as important self-care techniques that can aid in the grieving process.

Grieving is a highly individualistic, highly customized experience that is impacted by social groups and culture. Even if they are a close family member who shares the same home with you, their process of grieving the loss of a pet may look very different from yours.

The steps listed below can be used to nurture someone who is going through a very trying and emotionally stressful time. Our sorrow is an outward manifestation of the love we have experienced, the agony of loss, and the process of having to reintegrate our lives into what it will be like in the "absence" of our pet. "Absence" is placed in quotes as many people believe it is merely a physical loss and that our pets will always be in our hearts and have a lasting impact on our lives.

Emotional Care

We are in a period when there are always dozens of tasks on the "to-do" list and the capacity to only complete five things in a day. It is a time of continual distraction and rapid movement. Due to the unpleasant emotions on the inside, those who are grieving may feel irate that life hasn't slowed down on the outside. You need time to mourn and to completely experience your feelings. Allow yourself the space to feel your emotions at regular intervals during your grieving process, starting daily, especially in the beginning. If you don't, you can find yourself suppressing your feelings, which could lead to future pain.

One of the most important steps in getting through the grieving process is saying farewell to those we love. Sometimes, we don't get to say goodbye to our pets before they pass away. Some people may experience a hole in their hearts as a result of not receiving any sort of closure during this process. Making a memorial for your pet can help you find some kind of closure. You can build shadow boxes using your pet's tags, collars, and paw imprint, write them a letter, hold funerals and services, or all of these. Others decide to locate a special place from their pet's past and spend some time there. Remembering the wonderful moments and life that were shared can never be done in the wrong way.

We often grieve within groups even though grief is a highly personal feeling. Even entire communities have their own ways of grieving. Recognizing when you require support is vital during the grieving process. A cup of coffee or calling a sympathetic friend to go on your first walk together after the passing of your pet could be examples of this kind of support. It might also take the form of requesting assistance from a helping professional to cope with the sorrow and anxiety caused by losing your pet.

Physical Care

The complete loss of appetite is one of the most common problems during the acute period, often known as the immediate phase of grief. Sleep disturbances are also rather prevalent because our minds may be trying to process the experience quickly. It is also affected by guilt. As often as you can, try to keep eating. Additionally, make an effort to load up on healthy foods. Grieving requires a lot of effort and can be physically draining. Fill up on nutrients to aid with bodily processing. Try to keep a regular sleep schedule, go to bed at regular times, and pay attention to your preferred relaxing practices while doing so.

Cognitive Care

Animals prefer structure and routine. Your living pets are mourning the loss and absence of your passed pet and their companion at the same time that you are. Grieving dogs may look for a missing pack member. Cats may hide or spend more time alone, altering their behavior as they go through the same thing as you. Horses may whiny and run along the fence line for a while as they wait for their companion to call them back. To avoid interfering with either their process or your own, try to keep feeding and walking schedules. Although the first few times can be unpleasant, routines provide us with a feeling of order and familiarity, and over time, acute triggers can lessen.

Spiritual Care

Even for those who have never felt the agony of loss, active reflection can be challenging. Spend some time reflecting, whether it is through writing, storytelling, or another form of expression that soothes you. I urge you to begin your memory journey by reflecting on the life you two shared. You might want to immediately record your grief's pain, especially at first. However, try to start by focusing on the pleasant memories that were shared as you are taking the time to purposely reflect on your journey.

This gradually enables your body to feel a different emotion and aids in the transition from pain to gratefulness for the time you spent together. Be careful not to adopt this technique to avoid feeling pain; both must be felt during the grieving process.

We rarely get days off from work to mourn the loss of our pets, and even then, our employers are only required by law to give us three days off for the deaths of members of our immediate, human family. The anxiety that may rise during social duties when we are still grieving can be reduced by choosing a soothing activity like meditation, active concentration on breathing, mindful eating, or releasing our physical tension.

NATURE-BASED HEALING

Stepping outside can help us rediscover our natural well-being. Exposure to nature or outdoor scenery considerably improves people's moods. Being outside brings about a genuine sense of vigor. Our surroundings can have a big impact on how stressed we are. Our general mood can fluctuate depending on what we see, hear, and experience. Additionally, these factors have a significant impact on our immunological, endocrine, and neurological systems. A more pleasant environment is far more supportive of good physical and mental health.

When your beloved pet has passed away, these great advantages become all the more significant. Spending time outside provides a welcome break from the stresses of the mind. You can change your perspective and focus on positive thoughts, such as pleasant memories of the time you and your companion spent together.

The following are some benefits of nature on general well-being during times of grief:

- **Fresh Perspective:** Being surrounded by plants, soil, and trees serves as a constant reminder of the wheel of life. There is a natural sequence to things, and if you have gentle reminders like those that nature offers, you can find peace and acceptance.

- **Higher Oxygen Levels:** Taking some fresh air can make you feel better. Serotonin, a crucial neurotransmitter that influences your mood in general, memory, appetite, and other key aspects of your personality, has been related to high oxygen levels.

- **An Opportunity for Reflection:** One of the best ways to deal with the stresses of sorrow is to have a low-stress time remembering your pet. It is also good for your mood to meditate outside while thinking about your dog, cat, or ferret.

Muscle tension, heart rate, and blood pressure can all be lowered by exposure to nature. Focusing on the beauty of nature also reduces the release of stress hormones. Even something as simple as having a plant in the room can significantly improve feelings of relaxation. Additionally, the benefits of exercise in a natural setting, while grieving, help lessen the strongest emotions, such as depression. When you walk, hike, or run, your body releases endorphins, which make your mood and thoughts more positive.

Spending time surrounded by trees, water, and birds can make you feel more connected to the rest of the world, whether you live in a crowded metropolis or a less populated area. Having a sense of belonging can be very comforting at a difficult moment. A positive outlook will help you cope with mourning more successfully. Processing the loss of a beloved animal companion can also be made easier by developing greater empathy for your fellow humans.

GRIEF ART THERAPY

It's not necessary to follow conventional paths to healing after losing a pet. Talking to friends, relatives, or a professional can help you get started on the road to healing. However, traditional talk therapy is not the sole option for beginning your quest to rediscover joy. Because you are a complex person, you will discover that what works for one person may not work for another. Another way to find healing is through grief art therapy. But what exactly is it?

Grief art therapy is centered on creative expression and symbolic communication through artistic endeavors (such as painting or sketching), especially for those dealing with grief.

In other words, art therapy makes use of your artistic expression through a variety of media, such as poetry, painting, and sketching, to help calm and address feelings that are connected to sorrow, loss, or any other emotionally taxing circumstance. It is an effective method for providing a healthy diversion and a haven of calm and peace away from the distressing feelings connected to loss and grieving. After experiencing sadness, pursuing your creativity is a healthy approach to rediscovering happiness in your life.

Three Is Yellow

Both beginner and seasoned artists can consider this as an excellent alternative. You have several possibilities if you are adaptable and eager to try something new. Vintage vehicles, landscapes, animals, and other themes are just a few of the various ones available in paint-by-number kits. You can also get a personalized paint-by-numbers kit if you'd want to commemorate your pet. This is a fantastic opportunity to simultaneously try something new, have fun, and unwind.

Get Off to a Fresh Art

Speaking of painting, if you're seeking a new kind of creative art experience outside the home, think about enrolling in an art class. Various types of art classes are available, including sculpting, pottery, and painting. Again, you may use this art to create something to memorialize your beloved pet.

Create a Memory Quilt

Quilting is a more traditional art therapy exercise. Beautiful memories can be woven into a quilt to create a very unique piece of art. You can make your own memorial quilt, or you can check into beginner's kits and tutorials if you're new to it. You can go through online patterns and quilts that feature pet portraits. Even more simple no-sew quilt kits are available for children.

Need for Bead

You can make your own designs using beadwork, or if you're just getting started or need some ideas, you can find self-help tools and kits to get you going.

Stay Inside the Lines

An additional approach for art therapy is through adult coloring books. Yes, you heard me! Coloring is not just for children, but it will help you feel like a kid again. It's quite simple to color in the pre-drawn designs in the kit. It's a simple way to escape the present and think back to when you were younger, when your main concerns were things like making sure you ate all of your veggies for supper and that you colored between the lines. You can pick among many themes, including landscapes, flowers, or vintage autos. Try whatever your heart leads you to.

Visual Arts

This entails expressing your creativity by making something appealing to the eye. You can make a beautiful photo collage, try your skills at mandala art, decorate items (such as photo frames) or rooms, get a tattoo in remembrance of your pet, or pick up the needles and start knitting.

Performing Arts

You can get quite creative with performing arts. If you have musical talents, you can either play music or find out how you can record your music. You can also try dancing. If you already know how to dance, learn new styles like the tango. Finally, you can put your creativity to the test by making a beautiful or funny video.

Annette's
STORY

Sunny was a yellow labrador and what Annette calls a "concept dog." They did everything together. Since Annette loves hiking and spending time in nature, she always took Sunny with her. Apart from the last months that Sunny was fading because of cancer, she had a great life.

Her days were spent chasing Frisbees, playing in the mountains, swimming in rivers, sleeping on couches, and smuggling food from the table. She supported Annette as she handled divorce, single parenting, financial hardships, demanding jobs, PTSD, a mother with dementia, a father with Alzheimer's disease, and an empty nest after her son left for college. She was Annette's devoted hiking companion and supportive copilot. Given Sunny's lengthy and fulfilling life, Annette reasoned that she would be relieved when she passed away and was freed from suffering. But instead, Annette felt like she was falling apart.

She initially believed that being without a dog could mark a new chapter for her. She could now partake in social interactions that she had previously shunned because Sunny was either too ill or she preferred her company to alternatives. She went on lengthy day hikes in the mountains with friends, took road trips to big cities, and even tried dating again after a long absence.

But nothing felt right. Annette would often hold back her tears as she wished she could be with Sunny or at the very least know that Sunny would be waiting for her when she returned home. Although her friends were thrilled that she would finally start dating, she realized in her heart that this was not what she needed.

Although she decided against adopting another dog, she couldn't help but look at puppies online at 2 in the morning. That's when she found Trudy—an organization reached out to Annette, asking if she was willing to adopt this 138abrador. When she arrived at the place where she had to pick up Trudy, a neighbor asked if she was sure she wanted to do this. She replied, "Why wouldn't I be?" The neighbor said, "Well, she has some bad habits."

Annette rescued Trudy from a neglectful owner. This meant that she was not accustomed to spending a lot of time with humans. Trudy was not a "concept dog," but rather a "project dog." Still, a project Annette was willing to take on. Although Trudy doesn't have Sunny's personality, Annette accepts that she has her own unique and special personality.

After some specialized dog training, they are able to spend time together where Annette finds solace and healing from grieving Sunny—mountains and rivers.

Part of Annette's mind was still searching for Sunny, even when she was with Trudy. But whenever she was surrounded by the stunning beauty of nature, she always felt as though she had found Sunny—at least in spirit. Perhaps, this was a result of their mutual immersion in the wild as they traveled more than 15,000 miles together. As the Milky Way sparkles overhead, the tops of snow-capped mountains glow at dusk, or a fox appears from a bush and locks eyes with her, she can't help but think, "Oh, there you are" (McGivney, 2022).

Losing a pet is difficult and painful. But it's always important to take care of yourself, especially now. Embrace your pain in whichever way feels right to you. It's okay if you need to yell, sob, or just sit quietly for a while. Grieving is a process; there is no right or wrong way to do it. Attempt to follow a nutritious diet and exercise, even if you don't feel like it. Your physical and emotional health will improve if you take good care of your body. Avoid using alcohol or drugs to cope with your loss. These substances won't help you feel better in the long run.

The most important thing, regardless of your chosen mo'rning strategy, Is to give yourself time to heal and take care of yourself. These essentials for self-care can assist you in starting the process of recovering from and coping with your loss. Never forget that there is no one "right" way to grieve; instead, do what feels right for you.

But what if you can't move forward, no matter what you try? It is possible that you are being held back by guilt. In the next chapter, we'll cover how grief can influence your life, how to deal with it, and find redemption.

9

Letting Go

"Guilt is to the spirit what pain is to the body."

—Elder David A. Bednar

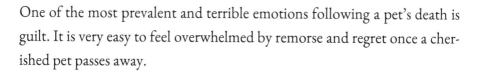

One of the most prevalent and terrible emotions following a pet's death is guilt. It is very easy to feel overwhelmed by remorse and regret once a cherished pet passes away.

- There are numerous things we regret not doing.
- We feel bad about all the things we could have done but didn't.

Because guilt entails irreversible actions, we frequently find ourselves blaming ourselves for things we can do nothing about for a very long time.

BREAKING THE POWER OF PET LOSS GUILT

Experiencing guilt for your pet's condition can result from feeling responsible, even when there is nothing a pet owner can do to change the situation.

When you learn that your pet has a terminal illness or injury, you could feel guilty because you feel that you should have detected your pet's symptoms sooner. Others feel guilty when they consider their finances or other personal circumstances when choosing a course of treatment. Others feel bad about choices they made or deeds they committed that may have exacerbated their pet's health. Whatever the situation, guilt has a way of obstructing you from processing your grief.

In this chapter, you'll find some strategies to assist you in overcoming guilt and letting it go.

Why Do We Feel Such Remorse After a Pet Dies?

First, we must understand that there is a difference between guilt and regret.

In general, guilt is a sensation of anxiety or dissatisfaction that you have because you have done something wrong, such as harming another person, or committed a crime.

Contrarily, regret is a sensation of melancholy about anything negative, incorrect, or a mistake you've made, along with a longing that things could have been different and better. It is to be sorry or upset over what you did or were unable to do.

The difference between the two feelings is determined by intent.

Many people experience the passing of a pet as a loss of a beloved family member who has been a constant companion and a source of affection in its most innocent and sincere form. The animals we share our lives and our hearts with are usually the only thing that holds steady and remains constant through all the changes in our lives. We go for walks, have conversations, have meals with our pets, play with them, exercise, and cuddle with them.

Why then are we repeatedly taken aback by the weight of our feelings when they pass away? Whether they can walk, fly, or crawl, have fur, fins, or feathers, we develop attachments to our pets, and the death of a companion like this can be devastating. You have the right to feel sad, heartbroken, angry, puzzled, or overwhelmed if your pet has passed away. In the mix of all these emotions, it is a small wonder that guilt would be included. In fact, all feelings we experience when a human loved one passes away are extremely likely to happen when a pet passes away.

Almost everyone feels some guilt when a pet passes away, even if the specific causes are different. The most common reason we feel guilty is because we mistakenly believe we have enough power to change the course of events. Similar to small children, we are often our pets' only source of food, shelter, companionship, and medical care. They may be able to show their distress, but they cannot pinpoint its precise nature or cause.

When a pet dies, it makes sense that so many of us feel as though we have failed in our obligations and are consequently unredeemable.

When Is Regret Over a Lost Pet a Good Thing?

Some people argue that the differences between guilt and remorse are meaningless because both emotions can make you feel awful after losing a pet. Because our thoughts can often trick us into thinking we're feeling guilty when all we're really feeling is regret, it can be challenging to distinguish between feelings for what they truly are. Despite how difficult it is, it's important to take the time to analyze whether you feel regret or remorse. You may gain useful advice from it about how to handle your mourning.

Guilt does play a constructive role in the healing process, despite it being difficult to believe, especially when it feels like a load that you'll never be able to shed. One must feel guilty to understand a situation and its circumstances. In some scenarios related to pet loss, we can gain knowledge from the questions that our guilt compels us to ask. In the future, for instance, we might cover electrical wiring after a pet chewed through them or we might change the lock on the garden gate after a pet escaped when the gate flew open.

We can learn more so that we can recognize signs of illness in our other pets as a result of our guilt at not recognizing the symptoms of a common ailment. All of these beneficial factors can aid in our ability to comprehend the passing of our pet and make appropriate future preparations, so the situation does not repeat itself.

When Grief Has the Power to Destroy

Unfortunately, guilt can overstay its welcome, taking up valuable mental space after a loss. Like a scab that you keep picking at, guilt can make you feel like you're stuck, reliving your loss over and over again without relief. This can also be extremely harmful.

You might conclude that you were a bad pet owner and that you shouldn't take in any more animals. Some individuals experience depression, social isolation, and confidence loss as a result of their guilt. Whilst having trouble falling asleep or desire to sleep all day, their appetite may disappear as well. Guilt can also be detrimental to relationships.

FROM CONVICTION TO ATONEMENT

Remember that making challenging medical decisions can be an act of empathy. There are many difficult choices to be made in life, and it is impossible to always know whether you made the right choice. All you can be sure of is that, given the circumstances, your pet led the best life imaginable. Your pet was fortunate to have a friend to look out for them, protect them, and love them without bounds.

Dealing With Pet Loss Guilt

Guilt is more than just a feeling. Guilt is fundamentally a conviction that we have done wrong and must pay the price for it. We must alter our beliefs if we want to overcome that conviction. These strategies can assist you in gaining the upper hand over guilt.

Remind Yourself of the Balance

Guilt keeps us focused on the times we think we failed, such as when we were "too busy" to play with, cuddle, or walk our pet. It makes us oblivious of all the precious moments when we weren't too preoccupied. Decide to refocus the next time your mind wanders to those unpleasant thoughts. Remind yourself often of the wonderful times you had as a conscientious and kind pet parent. Look through your photo collections. List the activities you engaged in with and for your pet. Make an effort to recall the positives. Recognize that a balance exists and has existed throughout your life between your triumphs and misfortunes.

No, you aren't entirely perfect. But you're not perfectly flawed either.

Decide to Accept What Cannot Be Changed

Self-imposed "penance" for past transgressions is ineffective. It only harms your future; it does nothing to right the wrongs of the past. Most likely, you've already made any necessary adjustments (like vaccinating your other pets). Can you make any other changes? Can what was done, be undone? Can you influence how your actions turned out? If the reply is "no," you can decide to accept it. Recognize that your future is the only thing you can change right now.

Decide Not to Dwell On Your Guilt

Do you often find yourself thinking the same guilty thoughts? They won't disappear on their own. To stop them, you must consciously decide to do so. Catch yourself first. Put up a mental stop sign whenever you see yourself straying down that hurtful mental path. As a physical cue to change course, you can decide to do something physical, like snapping your fingers. Then, purposefully concentrate on something different, like what you are planning for tomorrow. Concentrate on something positive in the future as a conscious reminder that there is more to life than the bad things from the past.

Forgive Yourself

It is not some esoteric theological ideal to forgive. In any relationship, it is an absolute necessity. Consider this: If you couldn't "forgive" the puddles, the torn curtains, the gnawed possessions, and the broken heirlooms, could you have had a relationship with your pet? Can't-forgive-you pet owners don't keep their pets for very long. In the case of your lost pet, it also worked the other way around. How often did your pet "forgive" you for ignoring them, arriving late, or yelling at them?

You need to make forgiveness the cornerstone of your healing because it has always been the cornerstone of your connection with your pet. If you did wrong, acknowledge it and extend forgiveness whenever guilt tries to remind you of it. It's okay if you made a mistake. It's done, and now it's time to proceed. Give yourself the same level of affection and acceptance as you offered your pet. You won't be able to recover and start loving again until then.

Sarah's
STORY

Sarah's beautiful black cat, Hedda, was 20 years old when she was euthanized. Sarah describes it as "the vet gently stopped my cat's heart."

She still couldn't get rid of the sense that Hedda preferred to pass away naturally and in her own time. Sarah had been clear that she would not choose euthanasia unless she thought Hedda felt that passing away would be kinder. She didn't think it was her decision to take Hedda's life. Nobody would probably look at a picture of Hedda compared to herself in her prime and think she passed too early. But Sarah was just concerned about whether Hedda thought it was too soon. She believed she had betrayed Hedda's confidence.

According to what Sarah heard, in this circumstance, we should take the course that will leave us with the fewest regretful memories. No regret is typically not an option with euthanasia. The best time for euthanasia is rarely obvious unless an animal is in grave suffering and there is nothing that can be done. Additionally, our resources and individual beliefs play a significant role.

In their final 24 hours together, Sarah made a promise to bear any unfavorable karmic consequences of her choice wholeheartedly, though she sincerely hoped there wouldn't be any.

Sarah understood that guilt is the mind's attempt to modify the past in a fruitless effort to oppose what has happened. Guilt keeps us from experiencing the full anguish of having to say goodbye to a creature we love, especially when euthanasia is involved. Indirectly, our mind makes up guilt-inducing notions like "I gave up too soon," "I should have," "I shouldn't have," or "I let my pet suffer for too long" to try to shield our emotions. These thoughts, which are the mind's constant dialogue, hinder painful feelings from leaving our bodies.

She has learned that guilt does not affect reality. Simply put, it makes us miserable. Guilt exacerbates the sadness since the heart cannot digest its grief while the mind is racing. She wanted to know that Hedda had forgiven her after she passed away. Sarah was the one who had to forgive herself since there was no other option.

Despite all of her internal conflict, she turned back to what she had been practicing for a while. Simply thinking that she should have acted differently can make her feel guilty. Sarah decided to explore that thought. She did this by working through questions from a therapist. Step by step, she came to a few conclusions and life-changing realizations.

These are the questions, with Sarah's responses:

Is it true that you should have done something differently?

Sarah answered that she was unsure. But she decided to say "yes," just for the sake of the exercise. She said that she felt she was utterly wrong to have helped hasten Hedda's death.

Can you be absolutely certain that that thought is true?

Sarah answered, "No, of course not."

Can you see a way the opposite statement might be equally or truer (i.e., that you absolutely should have ended her life)?

She reluctantly replied, "Yes," but there's a story behind that, which is that if that were true, then Hedda might have been in pain for some time, so Sarah wasn't completely off the hook.

What if this was absolutely the perfect timing, and you didn't do anything wrong? Could you see that as a true statement?

Sarah replied with a somewhat relieved "Yes." It was at this moment she experienced a huge energy shift.

If you didn't use up energy believing this thought, what would you have to feel?

Sarah's response was unequivocal. It would be "pain, loss, grief, and emptiness." This meant that it would be a lot simpler for her to divert her attention with more positive thoughts.

If you didn't believe the thought "I shouldn't have had her euthanized," what would you feel?

When asked how she would feel, Sarah replied, "Relaxed, calm, expansive, and grateful for our shared love and time together."

This succession of questions made Sarah feel less bound by her guilt. Not completely, but significantly. She eventually realized that feeling "guilt" was only a diversion from experiencing the agony and sadness, the quiet, and the throbbing in her chest. Because of the overwhelming guilt, she was also unable to appreciate the mysteries of life, love, and death.

This did not imply that everything would be perfect forever. She still missed Hedda's physical presence—even more so than she had when she had been using guilt as a diversion. But she discovered that each wave of grief subsided more rapidly since she was able to experience it freely, untainted by guilt.

Sarah's message is that letting go of guilt doesn't imply that we no longer love or miss our pets. Instead of attempting to change the past, it just allows us to experience the feelings we are experiencing at the time. It's okay if you are unable to control the onslaught of thoughts. Try to be as compassionate toward yourself as you have been for your pet. Feeling bad about feeling bad is an unnecessary layer of suffering to be added to grief (and guilt).

It's acceptable to seek professional assistance if guilt or grief are interfering with your day-to-day functioning. There are more and more in-person and online pet loss support groups, as well as one-on-one counseling choices. You are not alone (Chauncey, 2023).

There are several reasons we could feel guilty after the loss of a beloved pet. We feel a strong sense of obligation and love for the animals we take care of. As a result, it's simple to pass judgment and assign blame when a cherished pet dies. Additionally, we could experience remorse and find it very challenging or even impossible to forgive ourselves. If you are greatly disturbed by guilt and sorrow and unable to forgive yourself, the grieving process for your pet can become very difficult and can persist for a very long time.

Punishing oneself has no effect. Because it has always been the foundation of your relationship with your pet, you must make forgiveness the core of your healing. When guilt tries to remind you of your mistake, acknowledge it and ask for forgiveness. If you erred, that's fine. Now that it is over and finished, it is time to move on. The same love and acceptance that you would extend to a pet, do the same for yourself. Until then, you won't be able to heal and begin loving once again.

Once you've conquered guilt, the grieving process can proceed unhindered. A wonderful step in processing grief is commemorating your pet. In the next chapter, we'll discuss ways you can honor your pet's memory while finding healing and solace.

10

In Loving Memory

"At the blueness of the skies and in the warmth of summer, we remember them."

—Sylvan Kamens and Rabbi Jack Reimer

Nothing can completely prepare you for the passing of a cherished pet. Whether your animal companion dies unexpectedly or as a result of old age, saying goodbye to them might be one of the most difficult experiences you'll ever have. Even though you'll always have fond recollections of your time spent together, you may discover a special way to remember your pet long after they pass away. Commemorating the life of your pet can aid in the healing process and preserve the unique love you had for them.

PRACTICAL AND HEALING WAYS TO REMEMBER YOUR PET AFTER THEY PASS

Memorializing the life of the departed pet is one approach to dealing with grief. There are various ways to honor a pet, including ceremonies, funerals, volunteering or making a donation in their honor, or making a souvenir out of their ashes or fur.

Here are a few ways you can pay your respects and honor your pet's memory.

Hold a Ceremony to Share Your Pet's Memory With Others

Funerals and memorial services are effective methods for handling bereavement. A memorial is a deliberate act that can assist at the beginning of the healing process; it is more than just discussing or thinking about your pet. A customary method of saying farewell involves gathering close friends and relatives who knew the loved one and having them laid to rest. This method is equally appropriate for pets. A memorial ceremony can serve as a powerful reminder that you are not suffering in silence. Everyone can share memories of your pet and express their grief at your loss together.

It's not mandatory for it to be a public event if you don't want it to be. You are free to conduct your own private ceremony or service. When coping with the loss of a pet, some pet parents may find it helpful to lean on their family, friends, and community. If you find that your sorrow is excessive or prolonged, it may be helpful to address your loss with a counselor, psychologist, or other health professional.

Create a Pet Memorial Outdoors

Any form of aftercare that you select will work with this option. You could want to memorialize your pet by planting a tree or grave marker at the location of a home burial. If you opted for private cremation, you could also sprinkle your pet's ashes into the soil. You can erect a pet memorial stone anywhere you can view it or go to remember your pet even if you decide not to have the ashes returned.

If your pet was adventurous, a garden stone can be the ideal way to remember them. To help you remember your pet each time you pass by, you can personalize these with their name, a thought-provoking message, or a picture. Or, you might have their name engraved on a bench.

There are a variety of unconventional methods to incorporate cremated remains into a physical monument, such as services that let you combine your pet's ashes with concrete, which is then commemorated in the ocean as part of a living reef.

Plant a Tree or Flowers

Trees are a unique way to honor your pet because they represent life. Did your pet have a preferred spot to play in the backyard? A favorite park to go to for a stroll? Any of these areas is suitable for planting a tree to represent your pet's life and memory.

If you're unable to plant a tree, such as due to restrictions, consider planting flowers instead. A beautiful patch of flowers can serve as an equally powerful reminder of your precious pet's unwavering love and loyalty.

Preserve Their Paw or Nose Print

Making a mold of your pet's paw or nose can be a special way to remember them. This service is provided by many vet offices and crematoriums. Online stores also sell DIY kits that you can use to make an enduring memento at home. The finished product can be framed or turned into an ornament. Since the molds must be taken before or immediately after the pet's passing, preparatory planning is essential.

Alternatively, make use of an impression kit or ink pad to preserve the cute paw prints of your pet. The results can be framed and displayed, or you can just have them with you all day long by slipping them into your wallet or purse. Even though it's hard to plan this or you might not have the opportunity, you can try to capture your pet's paw print using ink or a simple salt dough. The dough print can be turned into an ornament, personalized artwork, a tattoo, or saved in a box with other mementos.

Utilizing food coloring is another option for capturing a pet's nose or paw print. If you think doing something from home is the best option for you, you can try this. All that is required is a sheet of paper, paper towels, a damp washcloth, and, of course, food coloring.

To begin, gently dry your pet's nose or paws with a paper towel. Afterward, dab the food coloring over your pet's nose or paw with another paper towel, making sure to cover the entire area. Then, to get the print, take your piece of paper and gently place it against your pet's nose or paw. And voila! Finally, clean your pet with a warm and damp washcloth.

Create Custom Art or Jewelry

You might want to showcase a unique piece of art that honors your pet. This might be a painting, a drawing, or even a sculpture made with some of your pet's ashes or fur. A lot of artisans specialize in creating distinguished memorial items like this. Any piece of jewelry can serve as a memento of your pet's life, but certain commemorative items can be crafted with your pet in mind. A little portion of your pet's ashes may need to be sent to some jewelers so they can incorporate them into the jewelry.

A pendan' or ring that can hold a small portion of your pet's ashes is an additional choice. A necklace can be as simple as a pendant that depicts their breed or fur color or as deeply intimate as a metal nose replica or paw print that has been specially made and is strung on a chain.

Get a Tattoo in Honor of Your Pet

Your pet has already made a deep imprint on your heart. Why not make a mark on your body to commemorate that connection? Of course, not everyone likes the idea of getting tattooed, but a lot of pet owners choose to do so as a way to remember their pets by getting their picture inked on their bodies. Some tattoo artists may even incorporate a portion of your pet's ashes into the ink, letting you carry a physical piece of them wherever you go.

With a personalized image, caricature, paw print, or nose print tattoo, you can pay tribute to your pet in a more lasting manner. The name of your pet or their silhouette are some other suggestions for tattoos as memorials. A tattoo is one way to keep their memories close, no matter how you want to remember them.

The Beauty of a Memory Box

Some pet owners preserve items with precious memories associated with them in a lovely souvenir or hanging shadow box as a way to honor their pets. You can recall the connection you had with your pet each time you see these items. Think outside the box and preserve some photos, a paw print, a lock of hair, a toy, or a collar to honor your cherished pet.

A memory box is a quick and inexpensive way to gather all of your best memories. It's a fantastic activity that kids may enjoy as well. Allow them to fill the box with sentimental objects like treasured photos, a food bowl, toys, blankets, and a leash. The box can then be stored safely in the house and looked at from time to time.

Commemorate Their Birthday or the Anniversary of Their Passing

Celebrating the loss of a loved one or pet on the anniversary of their passing and their birthday is an essential step in the mourning process. It is comforting to know that their influence will not be forgotten. It is also an opportunity to honor their memories and the times we shared with them. Some pet parents go to a place they both liked to visit or simply go through old photos to commemorate their late companion's birthday or the anniversary of their passing. This might be a once-a-year celebration to reflect on and express your love for your pet.

Give to Animals in Need

Giving back to others is a meaningful way to honor your pet's life. Visit your neighborhood animal shelter and offer your time to assist the homeless dogs and cats. You can also donate to the shelter in honor of your lost pet by sending supplies or money.

Contributions and volunteer labor celebrate your pet's life while also assisting you in your grieving journey. Owners can focus their intense feelings of love after a pet dies in productive ways. One method to channel that love toward those in need is by volunteering or giving.

If the organization where you adopted your pet was also a rescue, it may be even more significant to give back to them.

Kerrie & Isabelle's

STORIES

When Kerrie learned that Holly, her nine-year-old beloved pet spaniel, was dying last year, she thought that photos would not be sufficient to preserve her memory. So, an ICU nurse got in touch with Stuart, a sketch artist whose remarkably lifelike images are growing more and more well-liked among pet owners. As a result, Kerrie, who had Holly since she was ten weeks old, experienced great comfort.

Kerrie noted that Holly helped her get through a lot of difficult times in the last few years and that she will be sorely missed.

Thus, having Holly in her house as a work of art serves as a constant reminder of not only where she belongs but also of the companion Kerrie will always treasure. She claimed that Holly's portrait unquestionably assisted her as she worked through her grieving process because she felt that her dog was still with her in some special way. She added that Holly's portrait will always hold special meaning for her. She values it far more than just a picture because there will only ever be one portrait of her.

Clients often experience profound emotions when they see their lost pets memorialized on paper, according to Stuart, a self-taught artist whose most popular requests are for dogs. He believes that his realistic drawing style helps people immediately notice and connect with their pets. It's not like an abstract interpretation or an artist's perception, which may be off-target and very subjective.

That being said, Kerrie was not the only person who desired a painting to honor her cherished animal.

After her 18-year-old horse Sam passed away a few years ago, Isabelle contacted their local artist, John. She said that Sam entered her life at a time when she was truly having trouble with her mental health, and he assisted in bringing her through this tough time.

The entire family was distraught when Sam died. Even after many years, they still mourn his loss because he was such a significant part of the family. They had a ton of photos, but she stated they wanted something special and something unique that can be cherished by the family for a very long time.

She continued by saying that seeing Sam's image triggers memories and brings to mind happy experiences they had as a family, with Sam always at the center. In their living room, Sam's portrait is prominently displayed, keeping watch over them and providing comfort. Every time they take a look at him, they notice the stray hairs in his mane and smile to themselves remembering how they used to laugh—the moment they brushed his mane, he would roll or shake his head.

"Why wouldn't people merely put a photo on the wall?" That is a question that is often asked. Also, "Why create a portrait that is this photorealistic?" For John, the goal is to pique the interest of the audience. They may begin to study closely and try to understand how the artist accomplished it once they discover it's not a photograph but rather a piece of pencil art. This evokes a greater appreciation for the portrait (Bennett, 2023).

Building a memorial to preserve your pet in your heart and mind can help ease the unbearable grief of losing them. After a beloved pet has passed away, there are various ways to honor them, whether it be with a tangible keepsake, a farewell rite, or something else entirely. A thoughtful, personalized pet burial service can bring loved ones together to remember happy times spent with your pet and ease the grieving process. You are free to do whatever you want during the service, and it can happen whenever your family is ready.

Grief is a normal, painful response to losing a loved one. It's the price of loving someone. You can express your grief for this loss however it feels right to you. You do not, however, have to completely let go of your loved one. Relationships are still possible but in different ways—in your narratives, thoughts, and deeds. As a result, you may just discover fresh chances and new relationships.

Now that we've reached the next step on your journey to healing, we may have to address some issues that hinder your progress. Such a hurdle may be fear of the stigma surrounding grief. To overcome this, we must understand what grief is, exactly, and how it can affect your overall well-being. In the next chapter, we'll discuss the stigma and how finding professional help can do wonders for restoring your trust, love, and peace.

11

Fighting the Stigma

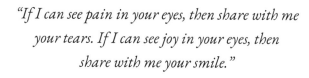

*"If I can see pain in your eyes, then share with me
your tears. If I can see joy in your eyes, then
share with me your smile."*

—Santosh Kalwar

The grief brought on by losing an animal is a particular kind of disenfranchised grief, one that is not widely acknowledged and is all too frequently endured in silence. However, a family's relationship with their pet is profound and complex; pets become a part of our life in many ways. They enhance our physical and mental health. They provide companionship for the lonely and solace for the hurt.

There are many small moments in this relationship that add up to something rich and significant, as they do with humans, making the depth of this relationship difficult to see from the outside. The diverse ways people deal with and mourn the loss of their pets are a reflection of this.

After having her 27-year-old horse, Cheque, put to sleep, Eliza discovered the grief connected with a pet's passing is rarely part of conversations. She decided to solicit opinions and personal accounts of pet loss from the public. What comforted them through their grief? The response was tremendous. She received more than 100 answers in only 24 hours. Patterns, coping mechanisms, and issues that people struggled with, mostly in silence, quickly became apparent.

Many respondents stated that keeping their pet's remains or belongings close by gave them comfort. Kim, Eliza's friend, lost her cherished chihuahua, Paris. Kim had her cremated afterward, and she now wears a locket containing some of Paris' ashes.

A whole industry has emerged to assist people in creating mementos for their deceased pets. Animal rescuer Bec kept her dog's collar as a bracelet until the ashes were brought home. She also constantly wears a locket containing pictures of her departed pets; three dogs and a budgie. Another animal rescuer, Sarah, spoke of the agony of losing her puppy. "I couldn't move," she revealed. "I was unable to get up. I could hardly even drink or eat. The pain was the worst, most agonizing I had ever felt in my life." His ashes are still kept by her bedside table.

Eliza asked vet nurse Kelsey what people do with their deceased pets. "Instead of a planned burial, many of our clients will request a cremation service or take their passed pets home with them," she said. Intriguingly, Kelsey also observed that when it's time to put a pet to sleep, owners frequently go to a different clinic than their regular one.

When we decide to put our pets to sleep, the pain that comes with their passing can get even more difficult. Many of us only have to make a life-or-death choice when deciding whether to put a pet to sleep. Because we are unable to consult with them about their preferences, we are forced to make this decision on our own, which may be extremely stressful and guilt-inducing.

The sheer volume of responses Eliza got—including images of graves, ashes, and deceased animals—seems to suggest that there aren't enough ways for people to express their grief. Although people recognize animals as members of the family, there is still a widespread belief that losing an animal is not a genuine cause for mourning. People discussed shame and guilt, with many saying they felt awkward asking for time off work even when they thought they needed it. More specifically, they felt that the people around them were poorly supportive of them. Most of all, people valued empathy, the knowledge that their pain was genuine and common.

Interestingly, Eliza discovered that the diverse and unique nature of the reactions showed that our society hadn't truly established customs related to a pet's passing. Some people preferred distance, while others preferred being near their pet's remains. People used tattoos, sometimes paw prints from their veterinarian clinic, and images to cope with their loss. They also used ashes and medications, as well as jobs and family. While we frequently see customs connected to a relative's passing, it appears that behaviors to a pet's death are far more variable (Henry-Jones, 2016).

WHEN AND WHY YOU SHOULD REACH OUT FOR HELP

Many people describe feeling disenfranchised in their grieving after losing a pet; this disenfranchised grief often develops into complicated grief. After a pet dies, the agony of loss can be lessened by empathizing with the person who is grieving and letting them know that their experience is understood.

Pet Loss Can Affect Mental Health

Losing a pet without receiving help during this difficult time can result in depression, rage, and other mental health issues. Due to owners' responsibility for a pet's welfare, grief also has some particular components, and people frequently struggle with guilt as well as feelings of loss for their pet. When a pet passes away, we experience a complex range of emotions: we mourn them, we worry that we failed them, we feel guilty for not doing more for them, and we wonder if we prolonged or curbed their pain.

There is a lot of guilt involved with pet grief, just like there is in human grief.

Owners may find it more difficult to grieve when their pets aren't cats or dogs, which are the most popular breeds in the United States. The loss of a dog or cat is more widely acknowledged and validated as deserving of grief, according to Michelle Crossley, an assistant professor at Rhode Island College who lost a guinea pig.

Adults who lack social support will frequently look to other pet owners for solace during difficult times. Although Crossley notes that some veterinary schools are including mental health and pet bereavement in their curricula, more veterinary professionals need to provide emotional support to pet owners during end-of-life treatment (Yarlagadda, 2022).

Signs That You Should See a Pet Loss Counselor

Throughout our lives, we all experience loss. It's an odd sensation because even though we all go through it; we often feel extremely alone. Grief therapy can help you feel less alone. Furthermore, it can aid in the processing of your grief so that you can go on. You can better comprehend how the loss has affected your life and discover ways to remember and commemorate the pet you lost while also making new plans and establishing new objectives for your own life. If you're debating whether or not you need bereavement therapy, know that it can't do anything else but help.

Let's discuss the signs that you may need grief counseling.

You Have Experienced Pet Loss

Counseling is beneficial for anyone who has experienced a loss. Of course, a lot of people experience grief without seeking therapy. It is a difficult thing to go through, but can nearly always be overcome with counseling. Before seeking grief counseling, you do not need to wait until grief has completely taken over your life.

There is no right or wrong moment to seek bereavement therapy. It's also important to acknowledge that there are numerous sorts of loss that people experience. Your sorrow might not be a result of a person's passing. Counseling is sometimes sought by people for grief caused by pet loss. Even though these grief therapy techniques differ, they are all equally crucial. You can profit from grief counseling at any point following a loss.

Your Work Suffers Because of Your Grief

Of course, after the loss of your pet, you'll likely be dazed. Getting back into the routine of things could take some time. However, if a few months have passed and you are still unable to return to a largely normal level of functioning, then you should receive assistance.

Grief counseling might be beneficial, especially if your performance at work or school declines significantly. For instance, you could want assistance if you failed a class or received a demotion as a result of your incapacity to function due to grief. Through counseling, you can both process the grief that is preventing you from moving forward and gain new skills and tactics to help you perform better at work while you process your grief.

You've "Moved On" a Little Too Easily

In other words, you're asking for trouble if you've avoided dealing with your grief in any way. The pain will reappear when you least expect it if you rapidly move on from the loss without actually dealing with it. Constantly claiming "I'm fine" is a crucial indicator that you're engaging in this behavior. You might say it out loud or just to yourself. Likewise, you are probably avoiding it whenever you try to minimize your loss.

Another red flag is if you start to avoid all traces of the pet you've lost. You remove their pictures from your house, stop listening to the radio when a song that reminds you of them is playing, and stop visiting the areas you used to enjoy together.

Or, You Feel Stuck and Unable to Move Forward

Unfortunately, grief affects everyone. There is no designated period of mourning. Some individuals begin to feel as though their lives are "back to normal" (or at the very least, a "new normal") quite fast. Grieving takes a longer period for others; therefore, to grieve at your own pace is acceptable. However, you might want to look into grief counseling if you start to believe that you'll never be able to go on.

The loss of a pet altered your way of life. Your life did not end, though. Grief counseling can help you break free if you feel that your life has come to an end and there is nothing to look forward to. Generally speaking, it is advisable to seek counseling if you have been mourning for a year or longer and still feel unable to move on.

When Your Grief Turned Into Depression

Depression is not grief. However, depression can develop from grief. You should get help if you start to experience clinical depressive symptoms. The following are some key distinctions between grief and depression:

- When you're grieving, you could experience death-related thoughts because you miss the pet you lost and wish you could be with them. When you're depressed, all you want is to stop hurting or to stop believing that you're worth living.

- In times of grief, you can occasionally experience joy, hope, and interest. You do not when you're overcome with depression.

- People who are depressed, typically feel numb or have a small range of feelings, whereas those who are grieving have a wide range of emotions.

- People who are depressed experience guilt, worthlessness, and low self-esteem. Even though you could occasionally feel guilty when you're grieving, your self-esteem is still intact.

- Spending time with those we love helps us feel better while we're grieving. With depression, that is not the case.

- Grief causes you to concentrate on the loss. When depressed, you emphasize yourself.

Ways Therapists and Veterinarians Can Assist

Counselors can assist clients who have lost pets by lending an ear to those who are suffering a disenfranchised loss. Before developing therapy programs for grieving clients, counselors and therapists must comprehend the significance of companion animals as well as the potentially devastating aspect of the loss. The more significant the owner and pet's attachment relationship, the more traumatic the owner's loss will be.

Although there may be some differences in how to process mourning for a pet-human relationship that was primarily non-verbal, therapists can employ the phases of grief to assist people process their feelings.

Some therapists include elements like anticipatory grief, in which people may experience shock and rage as they get closer to losing their pet, as well as self-blame when owners feel guilty for not providing better care for their animal companion. Nowadays, these approaches place more emphasis on acknowledging the importance of the pet-human bond and resolving pain than they do on providing closure.

SUPPORT GROUPS AND COMMUNITIES

The knowledgeable staff of pet loss support groups is aware of the struggles people go through after losing a pet. To help members of the community going through pet loss bereavement, many organizations offer monthly pet loss support group meetings. A grief counselor or another qualified individual usually oversees the online support group for pet loss. They will have a lot of experience working with grieving and loss, occasionally in both private practice and group therapy.

But how can you tell if a support group for pet loss is right for you?

Any adult with pet-loss-related grief concerns would benefit from joining a support group. Pet loss can take many various forms, with the passing of a pet being the most prevalent. These emotions could also surface if a cherished pet has gone missing, is stolen, or is diagnosed with a terminal illness.

How Other Pet Owners Can Help

People struggle to grieve on their own. Grief is meant to be shared, but because of the stigma attached to losing a pet, it could be more difficult. Nonetheless, others have also suffered a traumatic loss of that nature. Sometimes all it takes to process your grief and return to feeling a bit like yourself is just talking to someone about how broken you feel.

No matter how you choose to get through this trying time, remember that just because you're grieving doesn't mean your life has to be devoid of joy. Small pleasures or delights can help us cope with the suffering. So, make an effort to make time for your passions. Take a walk. Go for a manicure with a friend who also experienced pet loss. Grab a cup of coffee with someone you love. Even if it only temporarily relieves the pain, it's still an excellent beginning.

Think about it this way—in the same way you find support from this person, you can also help them with their grieving process. Just be mindful of what you say.

- Avoid using platitudes and euphemisms.

- When using images of the Rainbow Bridge, use caution because not everyone is spiritual or religious.

- If at all feasible, backup your claims with facts.

- Tell the story of your pet's loss.

- Share your memories of their pet if you knew them.

- Don't downplay the loss or look for a "bright side."

Finding a Support Group

Even if they are there for you, your family and friends might not always know how to help you in the best way. If you express your sorrow to others who have experienced comparable losses, you could feel less alone in your suffering. Listening to other people's stories can also teach you practical coping skills.

While expressing your loss to a loved one can be beneficial, if they cannot relate to the suffering you are experiencing, they cannot provide the support you need to recover. Many neighborhood animal shelters and veterinary offices provide counseling services and support groups for people who are grieving the loss of a pet. Spend time with other animal lovers who sincerely comprehend your loss or who are going through a similar experience. The connections you create and the support you receive when dealing with grief in a group can be quite amazing.

Join an Online Community

Online grief support groups have grown in popularity in recent years as a resource for people looking for knowledge and sympathetic people after losing a beloved pet. There are now hundreds of bereavement-focused Facebook pages and websites, and healthcare professionals need to evaluate what therapeutic benefits virtual communities could provide to assist people to manage their grief and come to terms with death. People who join these forums report less psychological discomfort, and this psychosocial benefit has grown over time, according to a study of online bereavement-support networks. People who had been community members for a year or longer described their mourning as being less intense than those who had only recently joined (Hartig and Voila, 2016).

It is highly beneficial to describe the pain that grieving brings from a psychological perspective. The internet can provide a safe environment for this to happen for people who might not have access to assistance or who feel uncomfortable letting those close to them witness their pain. You can find others who are going through the same situation as you online. You will be amazed at the friends you can meet in this way. Many animal lovers are eager to connect with other people who have similar interests. It can be tremendously energizing and motivating to know that someone is looking out for you, albeit in a different city, country, or even continent.

Online Resources for Dealing
With a Pet's Passing

There are a lot of support groups, hotlines, books, videos, and other resources that might be helpful. Consider the following support groups:

- Lap of Love
- Letters to Pushkin
- The Argus Institute
- The Association for Pet Loss and Bereavement
- The Companion Animal Association of Arizona
- The Two Hearts Pet Loss Center.

Inge's

STORY

As Inge was leaving the vet's office following the passing of her bunny companion Carmen, she came across grief counselor Marian's contact information. She was aware that she required assistance to cope with this loss because she had a history of depression. She was devastated by Carmen's passing and unsure of what to do.

Inge called Marian to set up a meeting on the second day after her passing. They connected right away. Marian even made the offer to meet with her that evening after learning how deep and recent her loss was. As a grief counselor, she provided her with the resources to deal with the guilt, emptiness, and despair during their sessions.

By sharing some of her own experiences and letting Inge express the hurt that was kept inside, Marian provided her with many helpful suggestions on how to take care of herself and her emotional health. The difference between feeling completely lost and having a helping hand through the grieving process was made possible by Marian's extremely personalized approach, attention to detail, and real concern.

Inge attended Marian's pet loss program as well and discovered that the exercises and guided meditations were able to access a level of emotions that she had previously assumed she had handled.

After that, Inge was quite enthusiastic about working with Marian because she and her adorable animal family were so helpful when she needed them (Testimonials, 2023).

The horrible sense of grief and emptiness that the passing of a pet companion leaves behind may be understood by anyone who has owned a pet and cared for it throughout their life. Understanding that grieving the loss of a pet is both appropriate and necessary is vital for recovery. Everybody grieves differently, but anyone who has lost a pet knows how important it is to go through the same process as we would for any loved one. And it's important to recognize and embrace the fact that sometimes we need help to process the passing of a pet. If you have lost a pet or an animal companion, it is okay to ask for support as you work through your grief.

How you deal with your sorrow after losing a beloved pet will be a very unique and personal experience. Whether it's a member of your family, a close friend, or your family pet, there is no right or wrong way to handle the loss. It's probable that you're unhappy, alone, or depressed. You might feel regret or anger. It is upsetting and can result in grief that lasts for months or even years when a pet or companion animal dies. If you find yourself overcome by sadness or depression or believe you need help moving through the mourning process, don't hesitate to seek the help of a trained grief therapist or counselor.

Once you have processed your grief to the point where you can see yourself loving another animal, you always have the option of adopting. In the next chapter, we'll explore pet adoption, when could be the right time, and what to remember if you choose to do so.

12

Adopting After
Losing a Pet

*"Until one has loved an animal, a part of
one's soul remains unawakened."*

—Anatole France

The most important thing after losing a pet is to acknowledge and process your grief. It can be quite tempting to run out right away and make a new pet friend, and in some circumstances, this can undoubtedly aid in the grieving process. However, it can also cause issues for both you and your new friend, therefore it is often advisable to wait a while.

In the end, there is no universally applicable "right time" for getting a new pet; rather, it is a personal choice based on several variables; some people even never feel able or inclined to get another pet. The ideal moment is essentially when you feel you have adequately processed the grief to be able to move forward and be enthusiastic about a new pet rather than continuing to obsess about your loss. There are still ways to interact with animals if you are not yet ready to add a new pet to your family, like volunteering at shelters or offering services of pet-sitting.

WHEN IS THE RIGHT TIME TO GET A NEW FRIEND?

One of the most essential points to keep in mind is that getting a new pet does not mean you are trying to "replace" or forget your previous pet. As a result, you shouldn't feel guilty or like a traitor; in fact, there may be no better way to honor your deceased pet's life than by giving another animal a second chance. You will be creating and enjoying a new human-animal bond rather than replacing the previous one since there are many animals in the world who need a wholesome and loving home.

Keeping in mind that your new companion is an individual in their own right and that you shouldn't expect them to have the same personality and conduct as your previous pet is crucial because doing so would be unjust to your new friend. Create a fresh, unique connection with your new pet.

When You're Ready to Adopt

You must first and foremost be prepared to acknowledge that you are about to resume an important role with a completely different animal from the one you previously had. You should also be aware that this responsibility cannot (or rather, should not) be taken lightly because returning animals to their previous owners is very draining on both the animal and the owners. Ensure that you are prepared to commit. Additionally, you must make sure that no one makes you feel guilty or under pressure. You're doing it morally and for your own benefit. Take the extra time you require and avoid comparing yourself to others.

In addition, be sure you are conscious of the responsibilities of caring for a new pet, particularly if they are young. Your existing animals may have adjusted to the daily routine and won't require as much babysitting, but a new puppy or animal may require continual care at first, along with training and other requirements. Will you have the time to spend bonding with your new pet, especially if it's a puppy? You want joy from your new pet, not feeling overburdened. Besides, the unnecessary stress will affect both you and your new companion.

Finally, consider whether you are prepared to make the financial commitment for pet expenses like food, toys, prescriptions, and insurance. Can you really afford all this? Additionally, will you need to adjust your living arrangements in any way to accommodate this new pet? As you can see, there are a lot of factors to take into account when getting a new pet. Otherwise, it can be a messy transition and not what you had in mind. You need to be in the correct frame of mind, have the time, be in a strong financial position, and have the ideal area ready.

Don't Be Hasty

Avoid making an impulsive decision. Allow yourself time to reflect. Don't let someone pressure you into making a decision that isn't good for you or rush you into making one. It won't be right for the pet if it's not right for you. A well-meaning friend or relative should not pressure you into deciding by bringing you a new pet companion when you're truly not ready yet.

Ensure That the Choice Is Shared by the Entire Family

Engage every member of the family in the choice to get a new pet. Take into account your children's wants and emotions in particular. Children develop strong bonds with their pets, and they could feel that adopting a new animal is "disloyal" to the one they already loved. Make sure that everyone in the family has had time to go through their own mourning process. Once everyone is on board with getting a new pet, discuss the best kind of pet to get. If at all feasible, let your kids assist you in choosing a new pet. You can also make it a team effort to decide where you'll adopt from. Give your new pet a different name (or nickname) from the one you gave your prior pet.

YOUR PET WAS UNIQUE

All pet lovers would agree—every pet has a unique personality, habits, and behaviors. It would be virtually impossible to find a pet that is *exactly* like the pet you've lost. And expecting them to be would only be unfair.

Keep In Mind That Your New Pet Is Not a "Replacement" for the One Who Passed Away

Don't consider the new animal a "replacement" for your earlier animal. Relationships are not replaced; rather, they are developed. You will create an altogether new set of memories and experiences with your new pet as a companion. Do look for a pet that is distinct from your prior pet in some manner. Choose a different breed or sex if at all possible. Avoid getting a "lookalike" pet since you can be disappointed when they behave differently from your prior pet, especially if they look similar.

Apart from avoiding the temptation to name the new pet after the deceased one, you should also resist the urge to adopt the first animal you see.

Recognize That the New Pet Won't Be an Exact Replica of the One You Lost

Keep in mind that your new pet won't be identical to the one you lost. Do not anticipate that your new pet will behave, react, or exhibit the same traits as your previous pet. Instead, take pleasure in your new pet's unique behaviors, responses, and traits as they emerge. Never compare your new pet with your old one. It is easy to forget that an animal companion was ever destructive, disobedient, noisy, or not housebroken, particularly when you have shared many happy years with them. Just remember that your new pet will move past the "difficult" stage soon.

Remember the Needs of Any Surviving Pets

Keep a close eye on your other pets in the days and weeks that follow the loss of your beloved pet. Watch for subtle adjustments in their behavior, level of activity, and appetite. If you lost a pet to a disease, make sure your remaining pets aren't exhibiting any signs of the illness. If you think your pet isn't feeling well, talk to your veterinarian. After losing a housemate, many animals experience anxiety and depression. Your veterinarian can offer guidance on how to help them recover.

When choosing when to get a new pet after one passes away, be sure to keep your current pets in mind. Some animals want the consolation of a new pet when they are grieving the loss of a friend. Although it might take some time for them to become acclimated to the newcomer, bear in mind that dogs and cats can be violently territorial. It's a good idea to provide your present pets with lots of love and care when bringing a new pet home.

For this reason, getting a new pet can be challenging for existing pets in your home. Think about how your present pets will respond to the addition of a new pet to the family. Animals take time to get to know one another, just like people do. Some animals need more time than others to become used to one another and not all pets will get along.

The attention your new pet is receiving may make your other pets envious. Make sure you show them lots of love and care to keep them from having their feelings hurt. Especially, if they still miss your other pet, they need your assurance that everything will be alright.

Preparing Your Home for a New Pet

Before bringing in a new pet, make sure your home has been entirely disinfected if your pet passed away from a contagious illness. Get rid of anything that might be contaminated, including toys, rugs, and beds. Think carefully about where to put your deceased pet's possessions. While some individuals believe that such items shouldn't be transferred, others like giving a previous pet's belongings to a new pet. If you'd rather get rid of your pet's belongings, consider whether a s'elter would be able to use those that are still in good shape.

A certain amount of space is needed for pet' to play, exercise, and relax. Furthermore, pets have a tendency to make a mess, have toilet mishaps, and get into inappropriate stuff. You might not have realized how much effort your pet was when they were younger if they were older when they passed away. Ensure that your home is prepared to house a new pet with a lot of lively, untrained energy. If you don't already have items like pet-friendly furniture, rugs, or tamper-proof food storage containers, you might need to invest in them.

Before bringing a new pet home, be sure that any pricey house furnishings or valuable objects are carefully secured or guarded against damage.

Sangi's
STORY

Sangi and Mellow only shared a home for around five years. Cancer claimed his (Mellow's) life while he was young. But he made everything so much more peaceful for Sangi and others around her. Because he reduced their tension, people wanted to pet him and be around him. He appeared to be everyone's favorite canine.

People would urge her to leave her door open so they could see Mellow when she brought him to her office. He was incredibly calming and provided a lot of comfort to everyone. He also helped her to enlarge her concept of family. These individuals all evolved into Mellow's aunts and uncles. And their devotion to him drew them nearer to Sangi.

But Mellow wasn't the first dog she loved.

Sangi had a guard dog as a child while still living in India. He was a German shepherd named Johnny. One day, he was taken in by those who pick up stray animals from the streets. He had strayed off and without a collar and was already gone when Sangi got home from school. Even though she was little, Johnny left a lasting impression on her. She continues to feel strongly about the plight of pets without homes.

Then, during her time in college, Zephyr, her best friend's dog, profoundly changed her life. He was a large, little too heavy labrador who constantly drooled and always overheated. He was a loving dog, though. Sangi also had the opportunity to experience what it was like to live with a dog. She's always wanted to be friends with a dog, ever since Zephyr. And a few years ago, her roommate from the time consented to adopt a dog.

A dog was brought over for a hou'e visit from the animal shelter. They had the feeling that they were adopting a kid. He approached the home and sniffed every crevice. After that, he sat down and sighed. They immediately knew: This is the dog.

That was Mellow.

Since he entered her life, Sangi's entire way of existing has altered. She came to understand that caring for another being anchored your day. That had a significant impact on how she lived her life, including how she formed relationships outside of the home.

She didn't only share images of Mellow on social media and speak about how adorable he was. She was aware that he awaited her at home. She thought about that constantly. He helped her feel truly anchored and at home in the United States. He got her to consider leading a purposeful life. Sangi always made efforts to do everything since she is an immigrant. Mellow effected a change. She had to live more slowly.

For him, Sangi, and others who genuinely cared about him, the last year of his life was extremely difficult. Despite being seriously ill, he made an effort to beam and make her happy. She had never witnessed a being behave in such a giving and altruistic way.

In February 2020, right before the epidemic, Mellow passed away.

Sangi was inconsolable. She needed time to comprehend the intense rage that accompanied her depression. But when Mellow died, the thing that held her day together died with him. Her friends thus encouraged her to adopt a new dog.

Sangi struggled with her feelings about adopting again. She questioned whether it was too soon. But living without a dog left a void in her life. Then the pandemic struck, which only served to worsen the situation. She then began browsing dog adoption listings online. She then noticed Iris. Her eyes had a certain quality. As soon as she looked at the photo, she knew this was the dog for her.

The agency first declined to place her with Sangi, since she fit the description of a high-needs dog. They lacked faith that a person who lived in a city without any other dogs could adequately care for her.

Sangi, though, was given a chance to watch Iris for a test run. Sangi and her partner were eager to pick her up from the foster home, but she fled before they could even open the door. About a day later, she was located sitting in an alley and brought back to her owners.

When she returned, she wasn't at ease. She appeared anxious and wanted to bite. However, Sangi is aware that anxious dogs can identify with her because she has ADHD and a high level of anxiety too.

Iris has taught Sangi a lot about herself since then. Iris was quite tense. Sangi, however, was able to learn safety thanks to the manner in which Iris did. Sangi survived abuse. She had a lingering fear from her ordeal. She had come to terms with the fact that she would never be able to do some things in life. But she found courage in Iris.

Sangi was able to discover that it's possible to find secure partnerships because of that change in Iris. Sangi was shown by her that she could overcome her ordeal. Additionally, she can escape even if she experiences recurrent feelings of anger or anxiety. She learned all those skills from Iris.

Iris has completely changed. She is truly gentle. She occasionally experiences anxiety, but when she sees Sangi or her partner, Sarah, she becomes calm. They are able to comfort one another.

Sangi has learned how to live a more conscientious life from both Mellow and Iris. She makes an effort to extend that to everyone nearby. She considers how trauma may have affected other individuals in her life. She always thinks of how she can show up and be a safe person for them.

Her partner's cat passed away just before they adopted Iris. Sarah found losing Frank to be difficult. They spent 14 years as friends. Iris, though, has really been able to support Sarah in her loss. They are now really close. They've even brought Iris to Frank's grave.

When Sangi considers what her dogs have done for her and what she has done for them, support is the first thing that comes to mind. In a world that encourages us to put ourselves first, dogs and other animals actually teach us what it means to depend on others. To find hope, healing, and peace in one another (Wiginton, 2021).

The most crucial step after losing a pet is to recognize and deal with your grief. Making new friends straight away might be quite alluring, and in some cases, doing so can undoubtedly help with the grieving process. But it can also lead to problems for both you and your new companion, so it's usually best to wait.

In the end, getting a new pet is a personal decision depending on a variety of factors; some individuals even never feel able or inclined to adopt another pet. There is no universally applicable "right time" to do so. The optimal time to move on and be optimistic about a new partner rather than continue to worry about your loss is essentially when you feel you have sufficiently processed your grief.

Conclusion

*"The holiest of holidays are those kept by
ourselves in silence and apart: The secret
anniversaries of the heart."*

—Henry Wadsworth Longfellow

Many of us have a deep affection and bond with our animal companions. For us, pets are more than "just a dog" or "just a cat," they're a treasured member of the family who enriches our lives with friendship, joy, and delight. A pet can give your day structure, keep you engaged with others and active, help you deal with life's obstacles and challenges, and even give you a feeling of meaning or purpose' So, it's common to experience overwhelming grief and loss after the passing of a beloved pet.

The sorrow following such a los' can often feel overpowering and can bring on a wide range of distressing and challenging feelings. You shouldn't ever feel embarrassed or guilty about grieving for an animal companion, even though others might not comprehend the level of affection you had for your pet.

The degree of grief you feel will frequently rely on things including your age and personality, the age of your pet, and the circumstances of their death, even though everyone reacts to loss differently. In general, the greater the emotional grief you experience, the more important your pet was to you.

The significance of the animal in your life can also have an effect. If your pet was a service animal, therapy animal, or working dog, for instance, you may be grieving not only the death of a pet but also the loss of a coworker, your independence, or your emotional support. Accepting their loss can be particularly difficult if the pet was your sole companion and you were a lone resident. Additionally, you might experience intense guilt if you couldn't afford to pay for costly veterinary care to extend the life of your pet.

While losing a pet is an unavoidable part of being a pet parent, this book addresses healthy ways to deal with the agony of loss, accept your grief, and, if the time is right, perhaps even open your heart to another animal buddy.

In Chapter 1, we talked about a true scientific animal frontier, which is the study of the relationship between people and animals, or our psychological and social interactions with them. The "human-animal bond" refers to the nature of our psychological and social connections to the other living things that inhabit our planet. Owners of animals benefit from having them, both physically and mentally. Pets provide us with unconditional love and companionship—two qualities that are becoming increasingly rare in today's society. Furthermore, they help to reduce tension and anxiety and even enhance our mood and mental health.

In Chapter 2, we discussed the different kinds of animal loss. Grief can be caused when a pet passes due to natural causes or euthanasia. Grief also occurs when a person is forced to give up a pet, when a pet goes missing, or when a pet is wrongfully killed. Whichever way a pet is lost, grief is inevitable, and the pet parent must work on coping with their grief on the road toward healing.

In Chapter 3, the topic of euthanasia was unpacked. Although this is a difficult decision, we must remind ourselves that we are showing our pet companion kindness. To know if it is "the right time" to put them to sleep, we must look at their quality of life. You should also prepare yourself for saying goodbye. After your companion has gone to sleep, you have the option of either a burial or cremation.

In Chapter 4, we found that losing a pet is practically identical to losing a loved one. The strong bond we share with our pet is often underestimated. Until they are gone, we occasionally don't realize how much pets influence our lives. The loss and void they once filled with unwavering joy and devotion don't hit us 'til they're gone. We spend a lot of time and money on forming unique ties with our pets, so it is only natural that we experience a profound sense of grief when they pass away.

In Chapter 5, we explored the five stages of the grieving process. These stages are denial, anger, bargaining, depression, and acceptance. Of course, acceptance doesn't mean we forget our pet, but simply that we accept the loss by facing and dealing with it. We never truly "get over" the loss, but we learn to live with it. It is crucial to understand the stages and how to navigate them successfully toward recovery and healing.

In Chapter 6, we covered how we can deal with the heartache after losing our companion. We have to acknowledge the reality of their passing, understand that every person grieves differently, that we must never let anyone dictate how we grieve, and that it helps to connect with other people who have experienced a similar loss. Mindful exercises can also help, such as mindful breathing, self-compassion, visualization, and not being concerned with a "deadline" for when we should be done grieving.

In Chapter 7, the subject of disenfranchised grief was covered. We often have our loss minimized or dismissed, as some people feel that "it was just a pet." We must remember that some people are uncomfortable dealing with another person's grief, they may simply not know what to say, or they may not be aware that we need help. Find ways to express your sorrow, remember that you're entitled to grieve, and reach out to others who have lost their pets as well.

In Chapter 8, self-care was the topic of discussion: how we can look after ourselves while grieving. We must take care of ourselves emotionally, physically, cognitively, and spiritually. Nature-based healing can be quite effective since spending time outdoors raises oxygen levels and helps us gain perspective. Grief art therapy uses creativity and art to navigate grief. Methods include paint-by-numbers, sculpting, beading, visual arts, as well as performing arts.

In discussing guilt associated with pet loss in Chapter 9, it was outlined that it is completely acceptable for almost everyone to feel some remorse when a pet passes away, regardless of the exact causes. The main reason why we feel guilty is because we assume we can influence how things will turn out. We are frequently our pets' only source of food, shelter, companionship, and medical care, much like we are for young children. It makes sense that so many of us believe we have broken our commitments and are therefore beyond redemption. However, we can improve and break free from this kind of guilt.

In Chapter 10, we dove deeper into the subject of practical and comforting remembrances for our pets. These can include holding a funeral or memorial service, creating a pet memorial outside, preserving their nose or paw print (or both), creating jewelry, getting a tattoo in honor of our pet, or creating a memory box. We can also give to animals in need by donating money or our time by volunteering at animal shelters.

In Chapter 11, we covered dealing with the stigma surrounding the passing of a pet. Many pet parents suffer in silence as they fear their grief is exaggerated or even "unnecessary." But just because some people don't understand pet loss, doesn't mean that it is not very real. The pain is not a delusion. If you feel that you cannot move forward, don't hesitate to speak with a professional. They are trained to equip you with all the tools you need to process your grief.

The final chapter detailed the possibility of adopting a new pet. To begin with, you must be ready to accept that you are about to take up an important position with an animal wholly different from the one you previously had. You should be conscious of the fact that this responsibility cannot be ignored. Ensure that everyone in the family is on board. Be prepared to go on a fresh journey with your new pet because your beloved companion who has passed on can never be replaced.

Now that you have all the tools you need to navigate your grief, you will find that you'll always miss your beloved companion, but that you learn to live without them. They'd *want* you to go on living, smiling, and being the wonderful person that they got to spend their life with. Your heart is big, right? Perhaps it is big enough to love once again. Even if a pet's life may feel "too short," you can make it rich with care, devotion, and unconditional love.

Did you find this book to be helpful either to yourself or someone you know who needed it?

If so, kindly leave an honest review. In this way, we can help other pet parents who need this book to work through their grief.

US	UK	AUS	CA
review.headuppress.com /ppoth.us	review.headuppress.com /ppoth.uk	review.headuppress.com /ppoth.aus	review.headuppress.com /ppoth.ca

May your pet's memory live on forever and may you find the peace, comfort, and healing you deserve. Truly loving a pet is one of the most unselfish things anyone could ever do—you *deserve* to find happiness once again!

About the Author

*"Our pets never truly leave us; they continue to walk
beside us in spirit, leaving pawprints on our hearts."*

— Nolan Sands

Nolan Sands is a pet lover and grief therapist who uses his expertise to offer comfort and strength to those going through difficult times following the loss of a pet. Drawing on his years of personal and professional experience, his empathetic and compassionate approach brings his recent book "Pawprints on the Heart" to life.

Nolan is renowned for his ability to put into words the very complex human emotionality, resulting in a profound yet enlightening narrative. He provides comfort to his readers and fosters understanding, addressing the deep and meaningful bond between humans and their pets. Despite the sense of isolation and incomprehension that often accompany the grieving process after the loss of a pet, its empathetic tone ensures that none of its readers feel alone during this difficult time.

Drawing on professional reflections and stories from other pet parents, his work offers a structured grieving process, allowing readers to feel their emotions and move forward in their healing journey.

A chocolate lover, Nolan firmly believes in the therapeutic value of a good book and a plate of brownies, preferably with a pet on your lap.

To keep up with Nolan's publications, you can follow him on his Amazon author profile and subscribe to the company's newsletter which is described in the next page.

About the Publisher

Head Up Press is a distinguished publisher dedicated to stimulating life-long learning, personal growth, and emotional intelligence.

This publisher proudly stands at the intersection of education and personal development. Instead of traditional, repetitive content, readers find diverse and carefully chosen topics that inspire reflection and transformation.

Head Up Press addresses a heterogeneous audience and arouses curiosity. From teenagers searching for their identity to emotionally resilient individuals forging their self-development paths, all find a home here.

Every word printed by Head Up Press has a unique purpose. It contributes to a larger mission: to empower readers on a journey of self-discovery. Each page is a step toward building emotional connections and personal growth.

Please learn more about Head Up Press at www.headuppress.com and join their book club to stay current on their latest publications.

References

12 pet memorial ideas to honor a deceased pet. (2022, November 11). CodaPet. https://www.codapet.com/blog/pet-memorial-ideas

A new friend. (n.d.). The Ralph Site. Retrieved June 6, 2023, from https://www.theralphsite.com/index.php?idPage=9

AKC Staff. (2019, August 6). *Grieving a pet: How to cope with the loss of a dog.* American Kennel Club. https://www.akc.org/expert-advice/lifestyle/grieving-a-pet/

Altru Health System. (2019, August 2). *20 ways to take care of yourself while grieving.* Altru. https://www.altru.org/blog/2019/august/20-ways-to-take-care-of-yourself-while-grieving/

Amatenstein, S. (2021, December 14). *How to cope with the loss of a pet.* Psycom. https://www.psycom.net/loss-of-a-pet

Anderson Allen, M. (n.d.-a). *Breaking the power of guilt.* The Pet Loss Support Page. Retrieved June 6, 2023, from https://www.pet-loss.net/guilt.shtml

Anderson Allen, M. (n.d.-b). *How soon should you adopt a new pet?* Rainbow Bridge.com. https://www.rainbowsbridge.com/grief_support_center/grief_support/how_soon_should_i_get_a_new_pet.htm

Anderson Allen, M. (n.d.-c). *Memorializing a pet.* The Pet Loss Support Page. Retrieved June 6, 2023, from https://www.pet-loss.net/memorial.shtml

Anderson Allen, M. (n.d.-d). *Ten tips on coping with pet loss.* The Pet Loss Support Page. https://www.pet-loss.net/

Anderson, T. (2021, September 13). *The guilt in goodbye.* Fear Free Happy Homes. https://www.fearfreehappyhomes.com/pet-loss/

Animal League America. (2014, February 25). *The stages of grief – losing a pet.* North Shore Animal League America. https://www.animalleague.org/blog/tips/life-with-pets/stages-of-grief/

APPA. (2021). *2021-2022 APPA national pet owners survey.* American Pet Products Association. https://americanpetproducts.org/Uploads/NPOS/21-22_BusinessandFinance.pdf

Argus Institute. (2020, August 1). *Moving forward after the loss of a pet*. Colorado State University. https://vetmedbiosci.colostate.edu/vth/animal-health/moving-for-ward-after-the-loss-of-a-pet/

Ariel, C. (2015, April 4). *The extraordinary bond between people and pets*. Theravive. https://www.theravive.com/today/post/the-extraordinary-bond-between-peo-ple-and-pets-0001853.aspx

Arneberg, C. (2023, March 3). *Why the bond between pets and their owners is stronger than ever*. Pet Honesty. https://www.pethonesty.com/blogs/blog/why-the-bond-between-pets-and-their-owners-is-stronger-than-ever

Ashes With Art. (2022a, April 18). *Why losing a pet hurts so much*. Ashes with Art. https://www.asheswithart.co.uk/blogs/news/why-losing-a-pet-dog-cat-hurts

Ashes With Art. (2022b, April 19). *What to do when friends and family don't under-stand pet loss*. Ashes with Art. https://www.asheswithart.co.uk/blogs/news/what-to-do-friends-family-dont-understand-pet-loss

Audacious Lex. (2018, August 3). *Rehoming your pet: Advice & tips (emotional)*. YouTube. https://www.youtube.com/watch?v=gMIx4H0T8wA

Bales, L. (2022, October 27). *How do you know when to put a dog down?* PetMD by Chewy. https://www.petmd.com/dog/care/when-to-put-dog-down

Barton, C., & Baron-Sorensen, J. (2007). *Pet loss and human emotion* (2nd ed.). Routledge.

Bass, L. (2022, July 7). *Nobody can tell you how to feel after losing a pet*. Self. https://www.self.com/story/how-to-cope-with-pet-grief

Baxter, J., & Lood, C. (2022, January 16). *New research confirms the strong bond between people and pets is a global phenomenon, 95% worldwide say pets are family*. HABRI. https://habri.org/pressroom/20220116

Becattini, F. (2022, April 20). *How to cope with putting your pet to sleep*. Neater Pets. https://neaterpets.com/blogs/news/how-to-cope-with-putting-your-pet-to-sleep

BeChewy Editors. (2023, February 23). *20 loving ways to memorialize your pet after they're gone*. BeChewy. https://be.chewy.com/coping-loss-pet/

Bennett, M. (2023, April 20). The pet portraits helping owners cope with their loss. *BBC News*. https://www.bbc.com/news/uk-scotland-scotland-business-65102829

Berg, E. L., & Causey, A. (2014). The life-changing power of the horse: Equine-assisted activities and therapies in the U.S. *Animal Frontiers, 4*(3), 72–75. https://doi.org/10.2527/af.2014-0025

BetterHelp Editorial Team. (2023a, May 12). *Guilt quotes to help you overcome and move on*. BetterHelp. https://www.betterhelp.com/advice/guilt/guilt-quotes-to-help-you-overcome-and-move-on/

BetterHelp Editorial Team. (2023b, May 19). *Pet bereavement: Coping with the loss of a pet*. BetterHelp. https://www.betterhelp.com/advice/grief/coping-with-pet-bereavement/

Bradshaw, J. (2012, November 19). *The bond between pet and owner*. Psychology Today. https://www.psychologytoday.com/intl/blog/pets-and-their-people/201211/the-bond-between-pet-and-owner

Brewer, E. (2022, January 20). *The importance of a pet loss support group*. Paws, Whiskers, and Wags. https://pawswhiskersandwags.com/the-importance-of-a-pet-loss-support-group/#

Callebaut, L. (2018, May 18). *Grief over loss of a pet*. Memorial Society of Edmonton. https://www.msedmonton.com/grief-loss-of-a-pet/

Calore, M. G. (2018, December 5). *Pet and owner: 5 key elements of their relationship*. Almo Nature. https://blog.almonature.com/en-us/pet-and-owner-5-key-elements-of-their-relationship

Campbell, J. (2018, October 4). *Coping with guilt during grief*. Sunset Vets Palliative and End of Life Care. https://sunsetvets.com.au/coping-with-guilt-during-grief/

Carr, S. (2022, December 8). *Grieving a pet can hit harder than the loss of a person, and that's okay*. ScienceAlert. https://www.sciencealert.com/grieving-a-pet-can-hit-harder-than-the-loss-of-a-person-and-thats-okay

Cesar. (2020, August 26). *How to cope with putting your dog to sleep*. Cesar's Way. https://www.cesarsway.com/how-to-cope-with-putting-a-dog-to-sleep/

Chauncey, S. (2023, May 2). *Euthanasia guilt: How to deal with your feelings*. Conscious Cat. https://consciouscat.net/dealing-with-feelings-of-guilt-after-euthanasia/

Cimons, M. (2023, January 31). *Dealing with pet loss: How to help a grieving pet parent.* The Washington Post. https://www.washingtonpost.com/wellness/2023/01/31/grief-pets-loss/

Claire, L. (2022, June 2). *Losing a pet.* Griefline. https://griefline.org.au/resources/losing-a-pet/

Clark, A. (2017). *7 self-care essentials while grieving the death of a pet.* Psychology Today. https://www.psychologytoday.com/us/blog/animal-attachment/201702/7-self-care-essentials-while-grieving-the-death-pet

Clements, P. T., Benasutti, K. M., & Carmone, A. (2008). Support for bereaved owners of pets. *Perspectives in Psychiatric Care, 39*(2), 49–54. https://doi.org/10.1111/j.1744-6163.2003.tb00676.x

Cohn, L. (2014, August 6). *Have friends or family ever failed you after a dog's death?* Dogster. https://www.dogster.com/lifestyle/loss-of-a-dog-pet-death-friends-family-failed-grief

Coles, W. (2022, November 27). *A new perspective on grieving loss of a pet.* Neuroscience News. https://neurosciencenews.com/grief-pet-loss-21950/

Connor, B. (2020, July 28). *Personal and health impact, coping, and self-care when your beloved pet dies.* Brynna Connor, MD. https://doctorconnor.com/grieving-the-loss-of-a-pet/

Coping with a loss of routine when a pet dies. (n.d.). The Ralph Site. https://www.theralphsite.com/index.php?idPage=80

Coping with grief and the loss of a pet. (n.d.). The People's Dispensary for Sick Animals. https://www.pdsa.org.uk/pet-help-and-advice/looking-after-your-pet/all-pets/how-to-cope-with-the-loss-of-a-pet

Coping with guilt. (n.d.). University of Florida Health. Retrieved June 6, 2023, from https://smallanimal.vethospital.ufl.edu/resources/pet-loss-support/coping-with-guilt/#:~:text=Many%20people%20find%20it%20helpful

Coping with sudden and unexpected pet loss. (n.d.). The Ralph Site. https://www.theralphsite.com/index.php?idPage=90

Coping with the loss of a pet: A guide for adults, children and surviving animals. (n.d.). In *Honoring the Bond Program*. The Ohio State University Veterinary Medical Center. https://vet.osu.edu/vmc/sites/default/files/files/companion/HTB/coping_with_loss_brochure_2020_web.pdf

Coping with the loss of a pet? A support guide for adults and children. (2021). In *Blue Cross*. https://www.bluecross.org.uk/sites/default/files/d8/2021-03/coping-with-loss.pdf

Corcoran, T. (2020, May 21). *How can art therapy assist for the loss of a beloved pet*. Pets and People. https://petsandpeople.com.au/art-therapy-for-pet-loss/

Cordaro, M. (2012). Pet loss and disenfranchised grief: Implications for mental health counseling practice. *Journal of Mental Health Counseling, 34*(4), 283–294. https://doi.org/10.17744/mehc.34.4.41q0248450t98072

Coy, W. (2016, February 22). *Making the heartbreaking decision to put your dog down*. SheKnows. https://www.sheknows.com/living/articles/1112153/when-to-put-your-dog-down/

Davy, J. (2014, January 21). *Why don't other people understand?* Pet Loss at Home. https://petlossathome.com/about/faq/grief/cope-with-pet-loss-others-dont-understand/

Dealing with grief. (2017, August 23). Pets in Peace. https://www.petsinpeace.com.au/support/dealing-with-grief/

Dealing with the grief of pet loss. (2021, February 15). CodaPet. https://www.codapet.com/blog/grief-support-for-pet-loss

Dias, J. (2009, March 23). *The experience of pet loss*. AKC Canine Health Foundation. https://www.akcchf.org/canine-health/your-dogs-health/caring-for-your-dog/the-experience-of-pet-loss.html

Dicconson, J. (2020, December 20). *Supporting those grieving a pet*. Goodbye Good Boy. https://www.goodbyegoodboy.com.au/post/supporting-those-grieving-a-pet

Dicconson, J. (2021, July 30). *Putting a dog down: 6 things to consider*. Goodbye Good Boy. https://www.goodbyegoodboy.com.au/post/putting-dog-down-when-to-put-your-dog-to-sleep

Dodgson, L. (2019, October 8). *Why losing a beloved pet hurts so much, and how to deal with the grief.* Insider. https://www.insider.com/how-to-deal-with-grief-of-losing-a-pet-2019-10

Drescher Johnson, K., Holt, S., & Scanlon, A. (n.d.). *Unconditional love: Grieving the loss of a pet.* The Parmenter Foundation. Retrieved June 6, 2023, from https://parmenterfoundation.org/wp-content/uploads/2021/10/Pet-Loss-02-After.pdf

Early days of bereavement. (n.d.). Living with Pet Bereavement. https://livingwithpetbereavement.com/early-days-of-bereavement

Ellis, C. A. (n.d.). *Coping with the loss of a pet.* American Veterinary Medical Association. https://www.avma.org/resources-tools/pet-owners/petcare/coping-loss-pet

Euthanasia ("put to sleep") and coping with loss. (2022, June 30). North Downs Specialist Referrals. https://www.ndsr.co.uk/specialist-referral-service/pet-health-information/miscellaneous/euthanasia-putting-your-pet-to-sleep

Euthanasia: Making the decision. (2016, August 25). American Humane. https://www.americanhumane.org/fact-sheet/euthanasia-making-the-decision/

Everplans Team. (n.d.). *What to say to someone grieving the loss of a pet (and things you should never say).* Everplans. https://www.everplans.com/articles/what-to-say-to-someone-grieving-the-loss-of-a-pet-and-things-you-should-never-say

Family-Friendly ways to memorialize a pet. (n.d.). The Ralph Site. Retrieved June 6, 2023, from https://www.theralphsite.com/index.php?idPage=96

Fantegrossi, D. (2017, March 21). *Why losing a dog can be even more painful than the death of a loved one.* IHeartDogs. https://iheartdogs.com/why-losing-a-dog-can-be-even-more-painful-than-the-death-of-a-loved-one/

Farricelli, A. (2023, April 10). *The stages of grief when losing a dog.* PetHelpful. https://pethelpful.com/pet-ownership/The-Stages-of-Grief-When-Losing-a-Dog

Friedland, S. (2015, January 26). *How to grieve the loss of a horse in 10 not-so-easy steps.* Saddle Seeks Horse. https://saddleseekshorse.com/how-to-grieve-the-loss-of-a-horse-in-10-not-so-easy-steps/

Gardiner, J. (2018a, December 18). *Journey of grief and loss.* UC Davis Veterinary Medicine. https://www.vetmed.ucdavis.edu/grief-counseling/journey-grief-and-loss

Gardiner, J. (2018b, December 18). *Self-care tips*. UC Davis Veterinary Medicine. https://www.vetmed.ucdavis.edu/grief-counseling/self-care-tips

Garner, A. (2021, October 12). *After the loss of a pet, how soon is too soon to get another?* CABI Digital Library. https://www.cabidigitallibrary.org/do/10.5555/after-loss-pet-how-soon-too-soon-get-another

Gayle, K. (2019, November 11). *5 tips for letting go of guilt after pet loss*. CPC Cares. https://www.cpccares.com/blog/tips-for-letting-go-of-guilt-after-pet-loss/

Gayle, K. (2021, August 18). *9 art therapy ideas for grieving pet parents*. Impurrfectlife. https://impurrfectlife.com/9-art-therapy-ideas-for-grieving-pet-parents/

Gilbert, C. (2023, April 18). *How a service dog helped with anxiety and depression*. Psychology Today. https://www.psychologytoday.com/intl/blog/heal-the-mind-to-heal-the-body/202304/how-a-service-dog-helped-with-anxiety-and-depression

Goldman, R. (2021, October 14). *How to cope when you're grieving the loss of a pet*. Psych Central. https://psychcentral.com/lib/grieving-the-loss-of-a-pet

Grainne. (2020, November 16). *Losing a pet*. Irish Hospice Foundation. https://hospicefoundation.ie/i-need-help/i-am-bereaved/types-of-grief/losing-a-pet/

Grief: Taking care of yourself after a loss. (2023, May 31). U.S. Department of Veterans Affairs. https://www.ptsd.va.gov/understand/related/related_problems_grief.asp

Grieving. (2021). Family Animal Services. https://familyanimalservices.com/grieving/

Grieving for the loss of a pet: Pet loss quotes. (n.d.). Let Your Love Grow. Retrieved June 6, 2023, from https://letyourlovegrow.com/blogs/blog/grieving-for-the-loss-of-a-pet-pet-loss-quotes#

Grieving the loss of a pet: Resources for coping. (2018, August 2). Best Friends Animal Society. https://resources.bestfriends.org/article/grieving-loss-pet-resources-coping

Griffin, J. A., Hurley, K., & McCune, S. (2019). Human-Animal interaction research: Progress and possibilities. *Frontiers in Psychology, 10*(0). https://doi.org/10.3389/fpsyg.2019.02803

Grossman, S. (2021, November 21). *Support, education, and resources for veterinary/animal caregivers.* Pet Loss Partners. https://petlosspartners.org/?gclid=Cj0KCQjw98ujBhCgAR-IsAD7QeAj9VexD-9LdJovKsEjPecLFRXjJdXXVo2Xn_-SZ_hNG1r8kodB-QGUaAq8xEALw_wcB

Hagen-Miller, L. (2018, June 22). *Why the loss of your pet could be the hardest to bear.* Healthline. https://www.healthline.com/health-news/loss-of-pet-the-hardest-to-bear#Should-you-adopt-another-pet?

Haley, E. (2019, February 25). *64 quotes about grief, coping and life after loss.* What's Your Grief? https://whatsyourgrief.com/64-quotes-about-grief/

Hammers, M. (2017, November 15). *10 ways to heal after losing a pet.* Everyday Health. https://www.everydayhealth.com/emotional-health/10-ways-heal-after-losing-pet/

Hartig, J., & Viola, J. (2016). Online grief support communities: Therapeutic benefits of membership. *OMEGA - Journal of Death and Dying, 73*(1), 29–41. https://doi.org/10.1177/0030222815575698

Healthyagingpoll.org. (2019). *How pets contribute to healthy aging.* University of Michigan. https://deepblue.lib.umich.edu/bitstream/handle/2027.42/148428/NPHA_Pets-Report_FINAL-040319.pdf

Henderson, E. (2022, November 25). *New perspectives to consider when dealing with people grieving the loss of their pet.* News-Medical.net. https://www.news-medical.net/news/20221125/New-perspectives-to-consider-when-dealing-with-people-grieving-the-loss-of-their-pet.aspx

Henry-Jones, E. (2016, December 21). The grief of losing a pet is traumatic and universal. So why don't we talk about it? *The Guardian.* https://www.theguardian.com/lifeandstyle/2016/dec/22/the-grief-of-losing-a-pet-is-traumatic-and-universal-so-why-dont-we-talk-about-it

Hines, L. M. (2003). Historical perspectives on the human-animal bond. *American Behavioral Scientist, 47*(1), 7–15. https://doi.org/10.1177/0002764203255206

Holloway, S. (2023, April 11). *Adopting a new pet after your cat or dog passes away.* PetHelpful. https://pethelpful.com/pet-ownership/Adopting-a-New-Pet-After-Your-Cat-or-Dog-Passes-Away

Holly. (2020, December 27). *Feeling guilty after your cat died? How to move on.* Large House Cats. https://largehousecats.com/feeling-guilty-after-your-cat-died-how-to-move-on/

How to cope with the death of your pet. (n.d.). The Humane Society of the United States. https://www.humanesociety.org/resources/how-cope-death-your-pet

How to memorialize a beloved pet. (n.d.). RemembeRing. https://lovingkindnessvet.com/wp-content/uploads/2020/10/How-To-Memorialize-A-Beloved-Pet.pdf

How to support a loved one who is grieving. (n.d.). University of Florida Health. https://smallanimal.vethospital.ufl.edu/resources/pet-loss-support/how-to-support-a-loved-one-who-is-grieving/

How will I know it's time to say goodbye? (n.d.). Lap of Love. Retrieved June 6, 2023, from https://www.lapoflove.com/how-will-i-know-it-is-time

Hughes, V. (2022, May 5). *When your pet dies, do you adopt another right away...or wait? (Part three).* Fox 26. https://www.fox26medford.com/when-your-pet-dies-do-you-adopt-another-right-away-or-wait-part-three/

Hunter, T., & Stoewen, D. (n.d.). *Loss of a pet - grief and bereavement.* VCA Animal Hospitals. https://vcahospitals.com/know-your-pet/grief-and-bereavement---loss-of-a-pet

Hutchison, L. (2019, April 17). *Coping with people who don't understand pet grief.* Centering Grief Resources. https://centering.org/grief-digest-articles/coping-with-people-who-dont-understand-pet-grief/

If your animal companion is shot or poisoned.... (2003, December 15). PETA. https://www.peta.org/issues/animal-companion-issues/animal-companion-factsheets/animal-companion-shot-poisoned/

Irvin, S. (2014). The healing role of assistance dogs: What these partnerships tell us about the human–animal bond. *Animal Frontiers, 4*(3), 66–71. https://doi.org/10.2527/af.2014-0024

Jackman, M. (2022, December 1). *8 practical and healing ways to remember your pet after they pass*. The Wildest. https://www.thewildest.com/pet-lifestyle/memorialize-pet-after-death

Janssen, J. S. (n.d.). *Helping clients heal after the loss of a beloved animal*. Social Work Today. https://www.socialworktoday.com/archive/exc_040215.shtml

Johansson, M. (2019, July 31). *5 signs that you might need grief counseling*. Maya Johansson, LMFT. https://wellsanfrancisco.com/5-signs-that-you-might-need-grief-counseling/

Johnstone, G. (2021, December 15). *How to know when you're ready for another dog after your dog dies*. American Kennel Club. https://www.akc.org/expert-advice/lifestyle/how-to-know-when-ready-for-another-dog-after-your-dog-dies/

Jones, R. (2023, April 23). *Ten quotes on disenfranchised grief*. Seven Ponds. https://blog.sevenponds.com/a-right-of-passage/ten-quotes-on-disenfranchised-grief

Jones, S. (2023, January 30). *How to know when to put your dog down*. Canine Journal. https://www.caninejournal.com/when-to-put-a-dog-down/

Kartini, J. (2020, August 12). *Getting a new pet after the loss of a pet: How to know if you're ready*. Pets in Peace. https://www.petsinpeace.com.au/getting-a-new-pet-after-the-loss-of-a-pet-how-to-know-if-youre-ready/

Kay, F. (2022, August 30). *15 tips for adopting a new pet after the loss of a pet*. Everlasting Memories. https://www.evrmemories.com/15-tips-for-adopting-a-new-pet-after-the-loss-of-a-pet

Kester Doyle, M. (2022, August 9). *12 unique ways to memorialize pets that have passed on*. Hella + Home. https://www.hellaproperty.com/blog/pets/12-unique-ways-to-memorialize-pets-that-have-passed-on/

Koenig, A. (2022, October 12). *The stages of grief after losing a pet*. Choosing Therapy. https://www.choosingtherapy.com/stages-of-grief-pet-loss/

Kogan, L. R., Packman, W., Bussolari, C., Currin-McCulloch, J., & Erdman, P. (2022). Pet death and owners' memorialization choices. *Illness, Crisis & Loss, 0*(0), 105413732211430. https://doi.org/10.1177/10541373221143046

Life after pet euthanasia. (n.d.). The Ralph Site. https://www.theralphsite.com/index.php?idPage=97

Linder, J. N. (2020, July 12). *The psycho-physiology of relationships: What you don't know.* Psychology Today. https://www.psychologytoday.com/intl/blog/relationship-and-trauma-insights/202007/the-psycho-physiology-relationships-what-you-dont-know

Linder, J. N. (2022, April 2). *The 3 reasons we love our pets so much.* Psychology Today. https://www.psychologytoday.com/intl/blog/relationship-and-trauma-insights/202204/the-3-reasons-we-love-our-pets-so-much#

Locker, M. (2023, June 4). *Why losing a pet hurts so much.* Southern Living. https://www.southernliving.com/culture/pets/death-of-pet#

Mader, B. (2019, November 25). *How do I support a grieving friend?* Pet Loss at Home. https://petlossathome.com/about/faq/grief/how-do-i-support-a-grieving-friend/#

Making the decision to put down your beloved pet. (n.d.). Rainbow Bridge.com. https://www.rainbowsbridge.com/grief_support_center/grief_support/making_the_decision_to_put_a_pet_down.htm

Martinez, N. (2023, April 27). *Helpful death quotes on the ways we grieve.* Everyday Power. https://everydaypower.com/death-quotes/

Maryruth. (2017, September 15). *Get out into nature: Let fresh air and raw beauty soothe your pet grief.* Tiny Pet Memories. http://www.tinypetmemories.com/articles/self-care/physical-response-to-loss/move-and-breathe-mindfully/a/get-into-nature-fresh-air-soothes-pet-grief

McAndrew, F. T. (2017, March 10). *Why losing a dog can be harder than losing a relative or friend.* The Conversation. https://theconversation.com/why-losing-a-dog-can-be-harder-than-losing-a-relative-or-friend-68207

McConnell, A. R., Brown, C. M., Shoda, T. M., Stayton, L. E., & Martin, C. E. (2011). Friends with benefits: On the positive consequences of pet ownership. *Journal of Personality and Social Psychology, 101*(6), 1239–1252. https://doi.org/10.1037/a0024506

References

McGivney, A. (2022, April 4). *What I've learned from loving a new dog while grieving another*. Outside. https://www.outsideonline.com/culture/essays-culture/pet-loss-dog-grief-attachment-theory/

McMahan, D. (n.d.). *What to say (and not say) when a friend loses their pet*. Headspace. Retrieved June 6, 2023, from https://www.headspace.com/articles/when-a-friend-loses-pet

McMillen, M. (2011, October 5). *After one pet dies: Should you get a new one?* WebMD. https://pets.webmd.com/features/after-a-pet-dies

Meaningful ways to memorialize your pet. (2021, October 1). Dr 4 Pets. https://www.dr-4-pets.com/blog/334143-meaningful-ways-to-memorialize-your-pet

Memorializing your pet. (2022, March 25). Funeralwise. https://www.funeral-wise.com/pet-loss/how-to-cope/memorializing-your-pet/

Milano, A. (2021, December 21). *8 ways to practice self-care while grieving*. Milano Monuments. https://www.milanomonuments.com/blog/6-self-care-tips-to-practice-after-the-loss-of-a-loved-one

Murray, J. (2021, August 26). *11 top tips on how to practice self-care whilst grieving*. Marie Curie. https://www.mariecurie.org.uk/talkabout/articles/self-care-grieving/315383

Nelson, S. (2017, October 11). *Grieving for a pet can take many forms and duration can vary, veterinarian says*. Kansas State University. https://www.k-state.edu/media/newsreleases/2017-10/losingpet101117.html

Neuer, J. (2023, June 2). *Self-Care during grief tips: How to create a practical self-care plan*. Eterneva. https://www.eterneva.com/resources/self-care-during-grief-tips

Nunez, J. (2022, August 30). *9 self-care essentials while grieving the death of a pet*. Wags to Wiskers Pet Supplies. https://www.wagstowiskers.com/pupdates/2022/8/30/9-self-care-essentials-while-grieving-the-death-of-a-pet

Ollila, E. (2016, November 16). *How to mix wet and dry food correctly*. Hill's Pet Nutrition. https://www.hillspet.com/pet-care/resources/honoring-memories-of-passed-pet

Ollila, E. (2019, April 2). *How to mix wet and dry food correctly*. Hill's Pet Nutrition. https://www.hillspet.com/pet-care/resources/animal-shelter-heroes-share-volunteer-experience?lightboxfired=true#

Page, A. (2023, April 21). *Pet loss quotes to help you through the toughest of times*. The Happy Puppy Site. https://thehappypuppysite.com/pet-loss-quotes/

Palma, D. (2014, May 12). *Veterinarian shares personal story of having his own dog put to sleep*. ABC News. https://abcnews.go.com/blogs/lifestyle/2014/05/veterinarian-shares-personal-story-of-having-his-own-dog-put-to-sleep

Pet Angel. (2019, May 16). *Coping with the loss of a pet*. Pet Angel Funerals. https://www.petangel.com.au/coping-with-pet-loss/

Pet bereavement. (2017). RSPCA. https://www.rspca.org.uk/adviceandwelfare/pets/bereavement

Pet loss support. (2022). The Anti-Cruelty Society. https://anticruelty.org/pet-loss-support

PetMD Editorial. (2022, October 27). *Pet memorial and funeral ideas*. PetMD by Chewy. https://www.petmd.com/care/pet-memorials-and-funerals

Price, E. (2023, May 26). *Time to euthanize? Use our when to put your dog down checklist*. Dog'sBestLife.com. https://dogsbestlife.com/dog-health/when-to-put-your-dog-down-checklist/

Putting your dog to sleep. (n.d.). Purina. https://www.purina.co.uk/articles/dogs/senior/saying-goodbye/putting-your-dog-to-sleep

Ramos, B. (2015, August 5). *6 stages of pet grief and how to move through them*. SheKnows. https://www.sheknows.com/living/articles/1089943/stages-of-pet-grief/

Reeder, J. (2021, May 19). *Why the loss of a pet is so challenging & tips for coping with grief*. Fear Free Happy Homes. https://www.fearfreehappyhomes.com/why-the-loss-of-a-pet-is-so-challenging-tips-for-coping-with-grief/

Reisen, J. (2021, August 6). *10 unique ideas for memorializing your dog*. American Kennel Club. https://www.akc.org/expert-advice/lifestyle/dog-memorial-ideas/

Reisen, J. (2022, January 13). *Is the human-canine bond unique?* American Kennel Club. https://www.akc.org/expert-advice/lifestyle/is-the-dog-human-bond-unique/

Renée, M. (2023, February 26). *The many faces of grief: How we all grieve differently*. See Beyond. https://www.seebeyond.cc/blog/2022/11/11/the-many-faces-of-grief-how-we-all-grieve-differently

Roldan, K. (2022, January 3). *100 best pet memorials when pawprints lead to Heaven*. US Urns Online. https://www.usurnsonline.com/pet-loss/pet-memorials/

Rutledge, K., McDaniel, M., Teng, S., Hall, H., Ramroop, T., Sprout, E., Hunt, J., Boudreau, D., & Costa, H. (2022, May 20). *Domestication*. National Geographic. https://education.nationalgeographic.org/resource/domestication/

Ryback, R. (2016, August 22). *Why losing a pet hurts so much*. Psychology Today. https://www.psychologytoday.com/us/blog/the-truisms-of-wellness/201608/why-losing-a-pet-hurts-so-much

Sabatini, P. (2021, December 24). *Expert explains unique bond between dogs, people*. The Columbian. https://www.columbian.com/news/2021/dec/24/expert-explains-unique-bond-between-dogs-people/

Saxerud, R. (2019, November 30). *Stuff no one tells you about dying pets: Guilt and relief*. Medium. https://medium.com/the-rac/stuff-no-one-tells-you-about-dying-pets-guilt-and-relief-241c54474eed

Schroeder, K., & Clark, S. (2019, December). *Traumatic pet loss*. The Society for the Advancement of Psychotherapy; Real Fun Art. https://societyforpsychotherapy.org/traumatic-pet-loss/

Self-Care while grieving. (n.d.). Essentia Health. https://www.essentiahealth.org/services/behavioral-mental-health-services/grief-bereavement-support/resources/self-care-while-grieving/

Seven heartfelt ways to keep your pet's memory alive. (n.d.). Animal Humane Society. Retrieved June 6, 2023, from https://www.animalhumanesociety.org/resource/seven-heartfelt-ways-keep-your-pets-memory-alive#

Shaik, C. (2023, March 22). *How to memorialize a pet*. Betterpet. https://better-pet.com/how-to-memorialize-a-pet/

Shailen. (n.d.). *A hidden sorrow: Experiencing pet bereavement as a disenfranchised grief*. The Ralph Site. https://www.theralphsite.com/index.php?idPage=91

Shailen. (2020a, March 28). *Guilt or regret? How the differences affect your pet loss grief.* The Ralph Site. https://theralphsiteshop.com/guilt-vs-regret-pet-loss-grief/

Shailen. (2020b, September 12). *How mindfulness can help you cope with pet loss grief.* The Ralph Site. https://theralphsiteshop.com/how-mindfulness-can-help-you-cope-with-pet-loss-grief/

Shailen. (2022, December 23). *When people won't talk about your pet loss grief.* The Ralph Site. https://theralphsiteshop.com/when-people-wont-talk-about-your-pet-loss-grief/

Shutterfly Community. (2019, April 16). *30+ pet loss quotes and words of comfort.* Shutterfly. https://www.shutterfly.com/ideas/pet-loss-quotes/

Silva, A. C., Ribeiro, N. P. de O., Schier, A. R. de M., Arias-Carrion, O., Paes, F., Nardi, A. E., Machado, S., & Pessoa, T. M. (2014). Neurological aspects of grief. *CNS & Neurological Disorders - Drug Targets, 13*(6), 930–936. https://doi.org/10.2174/1871527313666140612120018

Smith, K. (2022, August 24). *How to deal with grieving the loss of a pet.* Talkspace. https://www.talkspace.com/blog/pet-grief/

Smith, S. E. (2018, March 29). *When does keeping your sick pet alive become "too much"?* Healthline. https://www.healthline.com/health/end-of-life-care-for-pets#The-mindset-pets-as-family-may-lead-to-mismatched

Sobel, D. (2017, May 28). *Who provides care.* The Human Journey. https://humanjourney.us/health-and-education-in-the-modern-world-section/who-provides-care/

Soucy, M. (n.d.-a). *Dealing with guilt after pet loss.* Healing Pet Loss. Retrieved June 6, 2023, from https://healingpetloss.com/dealing-with-guilt-after-pet-loss/

Soucy, M. (n.d.-b). *Dealing with guilt and seeking forgiveness after pet loss.* Healing Pet Loss. Retrieved June 6, 2023, from https://healingpetloss.com/dealing-with-guilt-and-seeking-forgiveness-after-pet-loss/

Stages of grieving. (2017, June 5). Cornell University College of Veterinary Medicine. https://www.vet.cornell.edu/stages-grieving#

Stang, H. (2021, September 13). *9 self-care tips for grief: Reduce your suffering in mind, body & spirit.* Mindfulness & Grief Institute. https://mindfulnessandgrief.com/9-self-care-tips-for-grief/

Starling, M. (2022, November 25). *Profound grief for a pet is normal – how to help your-self or a friend weather the loss of a beloved family member.* The Conversation. https://theconversation.com/profound-grief-for-a-pet-is-normal-how-to-help-yourself-or-a-friend-weather-the-loss-of-a-beloved-family-member-195099

Storm, C. (2015, April 22). *Tender photos show the special bond between dogs and their owners.* Insider. https://www.businessinsider.com/photos-highlight-the-unique-bond-between-dogs-and-their-owners-2015-4

Stregowski, J. (2023, March 31). *How long after the death of my dog should I wait to get another dog?* The Spruce Pets. https://www.thesprucepets.com/getting-a-new-dog-after-death-1117496

Susan K. (2022, March 2). *The structure of love and loss.* Medium. https://medium.com/@33cadm/the-structure-of-love-and-loss-i-honestly-dont-know-the-origins-other-than-it-was-going-on-for-cbbabf0ecf46?gclid=CjwKCAjw6IiiBhAOEi-wALNqncXnUpuSE_YBF_Bghv57d7YZOmLIeI8nr_dPe9BXQn_okZSZ6gBi-4xoCXNsQAvD_BwE

Testimonials. (2023, March 24). Your Pet Loss. https://yourpetloss.com/testimonials/

The history of human-animal interaction. (2019). Encyclopedia.com. https://www.encyclopedia.com/politics/encyclopedias-almanacs-transcripts-and-maps/history-human-animal-interaction

The human-animal bond throughout time. (2018, December 7). The College of Veterinary Medicine at Michigan State University. https://cvm.msu.edu/news/perspectives-magazine/perspectives-fall-2018/the-human-animal-bond-throughout-time#:~:text=Pets%20need%20their%20owners%20to

Thodberg, K., Berget, B., & Lidfors, L. (2014). Research in the use of animals as a treatment for humans. *Animal Frontiers, 4*(3), 43–48. https://doi.org/10.2527/af.2014-0021

Tousley, M. M. (n.d.). *Loss and the burden of guilt.* Grief Healing. Retrieved June 6, 2023, from https://www.griefhealing.com/article-loss-and-the-burden-of-guilt.htm

Tousley, M. M. (2023, February 19). *Pet loss: When guilt overshadows grief.* Grief Healing. https://www.griefhealingblog.com/2019/08/pet-loss-when-guilt-overshadows-grief.html

University of Florida College of Veterinary Medicine. (n.d.). *Coping with guilt.* Hopewell Animal Hospital. Retrieved June 6, 2023, from https://hopewellanimalhospital.com/pet-bereavement/coping-with-guilt/

Valentini, K. (2022, March 10). *11 touching pet memorial ideas to honor your furry friend.* Daily Paws. https://www.dailypaws.com/living-with-pets/pet-owner-relationship/grief/pet-memorial-ideas

van Heeckeren, A. M. (2021, March 9). *Is it time to euthanize my dog or cat? 5 things to consider.* One Health Organization. https://www.onehealth.org/blog/is-it-time-to-euthanize-my-dog-or-cat-5-things-to-consider

Vasquez, A. (2022a, April 29). *How to Practice Self-Care While Grieving: Step-By-Step | Cake Blog.* Cake. https://www.joincake.com/blog/self-care-and-grief/

Vasquez, A. (2022b, June 8). *How to cope with an unexpected pet loss: Step-by-step.* Www.joincake.com. https://www.joincake.com/blog/how-to-cope-with-losing-a-pet-unexpectedly/

Vasquez, A. (2022c, June 8). *When should you get a new pet after losing one?* Cake. https://www.joincake.com/blog/getting-a-new-dog-after-losing-one/

Walas, M. (2021, December 13). *Grief associated with the loss of a dog.* The Living Urn. https://www.thelivingurn.com/blogs/news/grief-associated-with-the-loss-of-a-dog

Walker, K. (2020, December 18). *Surviving the hollow days after a pet has died.* Foothills Pet Healthcare Clinic. https://foothillspethealthcareclinic.com/blog/surviving-the-hollow-days-after-a-pet-has-died/

WebMD Editorial Contributors. (2022, November 9). *What happens when you put your pet to sleep?* (A. Flowers, Ed.). WebMD. https://pets.webmd.com/what-happens-put-pet-to-sleep

Weir, M., & Buzhardt, L. (n.d.). *Memorializing pets.* VCA Animal Hospitals. https://vcahospitals.com/know-your-pet/memorializing-pets

Werber, J. (n.d.). *The "new" pet: When is the right time?* Pet Health Network. Retrieved June 6, 2023, from https://www.pethealthnetwork.com/dog-health/end-life-support-grieving-dogs/new-pet-when-right-time

What's the difference between a pet parent and a pet owner? (2019, March 11). Big Dog Ranch Rescue. https://www.bdrr.org/dog-blog/pet-parent-pet-owner#:~:text=A%20typical%20pet%20lover%20is

When is the right time to get another pet? (2021). Patch & Purr; InvoCare Australia. https://www.patchandpurr.com.au/help-advice/dealing-with-pet-loss/another-pet/

When it's time to say goodbye. (n.d.). The People's Dispensary for Sick Animals. https://www.pdsa.org.uk/pet-help-and-advice/looking-after-your-pet/all-pets/when-its-time-to-say-goodbye

Whitehouse, P. (2013, July 26). *Heal after the loss of a beloved animal friend.* Mother Natured. https://mothernatured.com/parenting/when-you-loose-a-dear-animal-friend/

Wiginton, K. (2021, July 27). *My dog saved me.* WebMD. https://pets.webmd.com/dogs/adoption-21/dog-owner-mental-health

Wolfelt, A. D. (2016, December 14). *Nurturing yourself when you're grieving.* Center for Loss & Life Transition. https://www.centerforloss.com/2016/12/nurturing-youre-grieving/

Wood, T. (2019, December 8). Jewish philosopher Martin Buber says that an animal's eyes have free essay example. *StudyMoose.* https://studymoose.com/jewish-philosopher-martin-buber-says-that-an-animal-s-eyes-have-example-essay

Wulff Hauglann, M. (2021, May 4). *The amazing and true story of Hachiko the dog.* Nerd Nomads. https://nerdnomads.com/hachiko_the_dog

Yarlagadda, T. (2022, December 4). *We need to start treating grieving for our pets seriously — therapists can help.* Inverse. https://www.inverse.com/science/how-should-we-grieve-our-pets-therapists-can-help

Yonan, J. (2012, March 26). The death of pet can hurt as much as the loss of a relative. *The Washington Post.* https://www.washingtonpost.com/national/health-science/the-death-of-pet-can-hurt-as-much-as-the-loss-of-a-relative/2012/02/21/gIQALXTXcS_story.html

Zaleska. (2021, October 4). *How to grieve the death of a pet.* Health Essentials; Cleveland Clinic. https://health.clevelandclinic.org/grieving-the-loss-of-a-pet/

Zapata, K. (2023, May 18). *100 quotes about grief to uplift, inspire, and help you feel less alone.* Parade. https://parade.com/1089418/kimberlyzapata/grief-quotes/

Zinn, S. A., & Beck, A. M. (2014). From the Editors: The human–animal bond and domestication: Through the ages ... animals in our lives. *Animal Frontiers, 4*(3), 5–6. https://doi.org/10.2527/af.2014-0016

References: Images

Acharki, A. (2017). Man holding red and blue bird [Online image]. In *Unsplash*. https://unsplash.com/photos/zqDURGBpUvM

Alexas_Fotos. (2016). Horse, smooch, love for animals [Online image]. In *Pixabay*. https://pixabay.com/photos/horse-smooch-love-for-animals-1333897/

Arguello, D. (2018). He wasn't too happy that I woke him from his sleep [Online image]. In *Unsplash*. https://unsplash.com/photos/IQVxbAhPDqc

Bagacian, V. (2018). Man on green grass [Online image]. In *Pexels*. https://www.pexels.com/photo/man-in-white-t-shirt-and-gray-denim-jeans-outfit-on-green-grass-field-1314186/

Cagle, B. (2019). Long-coated brown dog [Online image]. In *Unsplash*. https://unsplash.com/photos/sg4Mw88fe_U

Cocoparisienne. (2017). Horse with girl [Online image]. In *Pixabay*. https://pixabay.com/photos/horse-animal-girl-woman-2644695/

Cong H. (2018). Calico cat on focus photo [Online image]. In *Pexels*. https://www.pexels.com/photo/calico-cat-on-focus-photo-1404819/

Hidden12saga0. (2015). Rabbit girl kissing [Online image]. In *Pixabay*. https://pixabay.com/photos/rabbit-girl-kissing-bunny-animal-949914/

Hughes, J. (2021). A dog with its mouth open and bubbles in the air [Online image]. In *Unsplash*. https://unsplash.com/photos/T0EddJ3PiXo

Lopes, H. (2020). Happy girl playing with dogs [Online image]. In *Pexels*. https://www.pexels.com/photo/happy-girl-playing-with-dogs-on-ground-4408935/

Low, D. (2023). Hachiko statue [Online image]. In *Unsplash*. https://unsplash.com/photos/uZLdpOdLOR0

Luciano, A. (2019). Mr Happy Paws [Online image]. In *Unsplash*. https://unsplash.com/photos/LATYeZyw88c

Pixabay. (2016). Close-up of dog relaxing on bed [Online image]. In *Pexels*. https://www.pexels.com/photo/close-up-of-dog-relaxing-on-bed-247968/

RDNE Stock project. (2021). Women comforting a sad woman [Online image]. In *Pexels*. https://www.pexels.com/photo/women-comforting-a-sad-woman-7951483/

Schellino, P. (2020). Man with white and black cat [Online image]. In *Unsplash*. https://unsplash.com/photos/uz4SEaiVWfM

Shvets, A. (2020). Cute puppy wearing a party hat [Online image]. In *Pexels*. https://www.pexels.com/photo/cute-puppy-wearing-a-party-hat-4588047/

Snap_it. (2017). Cute dog with ball [Online image]. In *Pixabay*. https://pixabay.com/photos/dog-ball-cute-pose-game-3010442/

Uschi_Du. (2018). Portrait cat young woman [Online image]. In *Pixabay*. https://pixabay.com/photos/portrait-cat-young-woman-face-love-3265622/

Vasilyev, M. (2017). A kitten named William hiding under a plaid [Online image]. In *Unsplash*. https://unsplash.com/photos/NodtnCsLdTE

Vuckovic, N. (2022). Doberman dog sitting outdoors [Online image]. In *Pexels*. https://www.pexels.com/photo/doberman-dog-sitting-outdoors-11497221/

Made in the USA
Columbia, SC
25 September 2023